THE PLEASURE BOOK

Books by Russ Rueger

The Joy of Touch
The Pleasure Book

Published by WALLABY BOOKS

Most Wallaby Books are available at special quantity dis-
counts for bulk purchases for sales promotions, premiums or
fund raising. Special books or book excerpts can also be
created to fit specific needs.

For details write the office of the Vice President of Special
Markets, Pocket Books, 1230 Avenue of the Americas, New
York, New York 10020

THE PLEASURE BOOK

Dr. Russ A. Rueger

Photographs by
Trudy Schlachter

A WALLABY BOOK
Published by Pocket Books
New York

To my brother Anthony,
whose unwavering belief in myself
and this project
lent me unlimited strength,
perseverance and drive
during moments of doubt

Another *Original* publication of WALLABY BOOKS

A Wallaby Book published by
POCKET BOOKS, a division of Simon & Schuster, Inc.
1230 Avenue of the Americas, New York, N.Y. 10020

ISBN: 0-671-50493-2

First Wallaby Books printing November, 1984

10 9 8 7 6 5 4 3 2 1

WALLABY and colophon are registered trademarks
of Simon & Schuster, Inc.

Printed in the U.S.A.

CONTENTS

	Preface	7
1	*The Psychology of Pleasure*	9
2	*Peak Experiences and Self-Actualization*	19
3	*Pleasure Prohibitions*	23
4	*The Pleasure Philosophy*	29
5	*Mental Pleasure*	37
6	*Work*	45
7	*Success and Achievement*	53
8	*Friendship*	59
9	*Love*	65
10	*The Healthy Hedonist*	73
11	*Recreation and Relaxation*	79
12	*Bodywork*	87
13	*The Beauty Quest*	95
14	*Psychic Pleasure*	101
15	*Spiritual Pleasure*	107
16	*Sensual Pleasure—Touch*	113
17	*Sensual Pleasure—Other Senses*	121
18	*Sexual Attitudes*	129
19	*Sexual Pleasure*	135
20	*Pleasure Products*	141
21	*Other Pleasure Pursuits*	149
22	*The Politics of Pleasure*	155
	Bibliography	159

PREFACE

While researching the predecessor to this book, the internationally acclaimed *The Joy of Touch* (Simon & Schuster, New York, 1981), I studied the different healing methods available, including classic Swedish massage. While reading Gordon Inkeles's popular book, *The New Massage* (Putnam, New York, 1980), I was intrigued by Inkeles's discussion of "pleasure as therapy." Inkeles's idea made complete sense to me. Very simply, feeling good was therapeutic for people. It made them less frustrated and uptight, and therefore lessened the likelihood of their engaging in violent or antisocial actions. It occurred to me that perhaps world peace could exist if everyone received a rejuvenating, relaxing daily massage or other regular pleasure experience.

A San Francisco sex therapist, Dr. Ray Stubbs, visited me after hearing about *The Joy of Touch*. Dr. Stubbs runs a unique training program called "The Gift of Pleasure," which utilizes techniques similar to those in my own book. He teaches people how to experience the wonder, magic and beauty of their bodies.

After speaking with Dr. Stubbs, I felt that my notion of writing a "pleasure book" was an idea whose time had come. The steady erosion of Puritanical restrictions—as witnessed by the nationwide explosion of workshops on sex, sensualism and other sensory experiences—clearly supported my conviction that the time was ripe for a book on the pleasure experience, a collection of "pleasure practices" much like *The Joy of Touch*'s "touch techniques." I approached a number of publishers with my proposal, and was finally commissioned by Leon Garry, publisher of *Gallery* magazine, to do an extensive study on the subject. That was published in 1983 as a *Gallery* special issue, *The Pleasure Book*, parts of which are included here. But while that *Pleasure Book* mainly focused on the sexual and sensual, this new *Pleasure Book* extends the concept of pleasure to entirely new realms, including work, success and friendship. In fact, the manuscript developed into a manual for spiritual enlightenment, a guidebook for psychological soundness, a handbook for physical fitness and a course in healing, while still maintaining its firm grounding in the wonders of physical, sensual and sexual pleasure. Since "pleasure of the mind" emerged as such an important topic, I also included one of the most extensive bibliographies ever compiled on all phases of the pleasure experience. I decided to make full use of my credentials in psychology, law and religion to take this book beyond a mere "fun and games" approach to a total mental, physical and spiritual guide.

Special thanks go to Leon Garry of *Gallery* for proceeding with their *Pleasure Book* when other publishers balked, and to Simon & Schuster publisher Jack Artenstein and editor-in-chief Melissa Newman for recognizing the merits of *The Pleasure Book*. And of course, the sensitivity and skill of photographer Trudy Schlachter must also be acknowledged. Thinkers who've lent me special insights have been mentioned in the text or bibliography. And since pleasure is not so much an abstraction as a living experience, thanks must also go to the many friends and lovers who've brought pleasure into my personal life, especially childhood comrades John Capraro and Annette Ponzo, who've stood close by me throughout countless triumphs and tragedies.

1

The Psychology of Pleasure

Your body was built for pleasure. All of your senses are finely tuned to feeling good. Our minds are pleasure-seeking mechanisms. We naturally gravitate to comfort, warmth and security, and, just as naturally, avoid pain and discomfort. Our bodies come equipped with an innate "pleasure drive," a built-in need to seek enjoyable experiences. Our desire for pleasure is virtually limitless. Advertisers are well aware of this, and they cater to our pleasure propensities whenever possible. They tempt us to buy their wares with sex, sensual seductions, love and countless other promises of ecstasy.

Sigmund Freud, the master of modern psychology, based many of his insightful theories on the "pleasure principle." Freud felt that man's subconscious mind was compelled by a primitive, pleasure-seeking drive. This innate force blindly seeks gratification and is only restrained by civilization and its behavior codes. Freud believed much of the discontent and anguish of modern life could be traced to society's constraints upon the pleasure principle, which eventually became internalized in the psyche, making them doubly difficult to deal with.

Other social observers have agreed with Freud's view about the need to drive the pleasure instincts underground. Moralists, religious crusaders, politicians and philosophers have warned of the dire consequences resulting from the relaxation of these rigid restraints. For example, antiobscenity opponents throughout history have cried that the legalization of pornography would unleash social chaos and rampant immorality, that we would all sink into a sea of depravity and life would decay into one long Roman orgy. They insist we must impose strict censorship and a rigidly enforced moral code, or society will fall apart at the seams.

Fortunately, more enlightened thinkers disagree. Many observers feel that society can only gain from loosening its restrictions. They believe a more tolerant social atmosphere will not only result in greater pleasure opportunities for all, but can contribute to enhanced creativity, intellectual freedom and self-expression. The philosopher Herbert Marcuse envisioned a society of nonrepression, one based upon the pleasure principle. In such a utopia, pleasure pursuits will be intimately connected with traditional forms of social endeavors. Pleasure will not be restricted to recreation and leisure, but will permeate all aspects of existence, including work.

Apart from the social aspects of pleasure, recent research reveals that our brains are equipped with natural pleasure substances. The limbic lobe of the brain, a primitive area associated with instincts and emotions, contains a high concentration of naturally occurring opiates. These substances, called "endorphins," are triggered in response to physical and psychological stress. The endorphins reduce blood pressure, slow respiration and relax motor activity throughout the body. They serve as natural pain-killers. Interestingly, they're also released in response

to exercise, which is why regular workouts are highly recommended for the serious pleasure-seeker (see Chapter X: The Healthy Hedonist).

We see now that the mind not only seeks pleasure externally, but also that the brain supplies its own internal pleasure stimuli. The senses are also very keen pleasure tools. Each is highly receptive to the pleasure experience in its own unique way. Touch, the first sense to develop, is probably the pleasure king. Our tactile abilities allow us to experience all types of sensual and sexual thrills. Cuddling, tickling, kissing, lovemaking and stroking are just some of the ways that touch can soothe and satisfy our pleasure drive.

Sight is another fantastic pleasure receptor enabling us to perceive the ultimate in physical and aesthetic beauty. With sight we can appreciate the wonders of the world, its majesty, its countless varieties of sizes, shapes and colors. The multiple marvels of nature—flora and fauna, mountains and oceans, rivers and forests— are revealed to us through the vistas of sight.

THE PLEASURE BOOK

Hearing also opens up pleasure avenues for us. Beautiful sights are matched by their enchanting sounds. Everywhere we go, our ears pick up the vibrations of matter floating around us. Nature provides a plethora of interesting noises: babbling brooks, the echoes of canyons and the rustling of windswept bushes. Man has taken the magic of sound even further with the creation of music. In music, harmony, melody and rhythm combine to produce exciting sensations in the body, making your pulse pound with the beat. The human voice is another entrancing stimulus for our hearing centers.

The sense of smell provokes many unique pleasurable sensations. Nature herself exudes numerous alluring scents for our enjoyment. Who is not captivated by the sweet smell of flowers, the fresh scent of forests, the salty smell of sea breezes? The smell of tempting food stimulates us to salivate hungrily, while the wonderful scents of perfume foster our romantic moods. Our bodies come equipped with many natural odors which pleasantly provoke our sensual sensitivities. Our nasal sense is surely one of the most earthy, primal sensibilities.

And finally, there is taste. This may be the most intimate sense of all. Taste turns a pure survival instinct, eating, into one of life's great enjoyments. Our taste buds are equipped to enjoy all types of flavors: saltiness, sweetness and sourness. We thrill at the varied temperatures and textures of food, as well as at the variations between solids and liquids. We can sharpen our taste perceptions and become connoisseurs of fine wines, or gourmets of fancy foods. The diversity of sensations our palates afford is virtually unlimited.

While each sense individually opens up a world of special pleasure perceptions, using a combination of senses provides even more heightened enjoyment. For example, a stereo system allows you to enjoy excellent sound stimulation, but a live concert adds an additional dimension. The live experience initiates visual as well as auditory stimuli, not to mention the excitement of being amidst an audi-

ence. There are many creative ways to merge the senses to provide maximum pleasure and potency.

Touch and taste make marvelous sensory music together in lovemaking. While enjoying the tactile thrills of your lover's body, you can nibble, kiss and lick many sensitive body spots like the shoulders, neck, face and thighs. Smell can also be creatively employed during sex. You can enjoy the scent of clean skin, the earthy odors of natural erotic secretions, and the delicate smells of perfume, powder and cologne. Your auditory sense will be enhanced by playing romantic or sensual music while in bed and the sounds of your lover's whispers, cries, moans and sighs will be music to your ears.

Your eyes will also be turned on as you watch the graceful movements of your lover, his smooth rhythms, and the gentle way he caresses you. You'll marvel at the sight of his different body parts, the various shapes, contours and textures, the diversity of organs, including the contrast between "innocent" spots and erotic zones. You'll also thrill at seeing the rhythmic movements of your bodies at the exquisite moment of sexual union. Then, you can serenely relax in your lover's embrace, exchanging loving, admiring glances.

Sex naturally provides almost limitless opportunities for an orgy of sense stimulations, but there are also many other opportunities for creative combinations. Taste and smell are inseparable brothers in pleasure, since part of the enjoyment of taste lies in the smell of food. Sight and sound are also ideal partners, as evidenced by the proliferation of so many inventions which combine the two, like television, film and video games. Sound and smell, and taste and sight are also complementary. Actually, the only limitations for combining lavish sense smorgasbords lie in one's own imagination.

Both our minds and bodies are marvelously equipped for maximum pleasure enjoyment. But the pleasure drive has a flip side, pain avoidance. We are not only programmed to actively seek pleasure, but also to remove ourselves from painful stimuli whenever possible. Actually, full enjoyment of our pleasure receptors requires us to mitigate discomfort as much as we can.

For example, if a man were about to treat a woman to a sensual massage, he should make sure that the setting is as comfy and cozy as possible. Is she warm enough? Is there sufficient padding underneath her? Are there towels and sheets available to soak up excess massage oil? Is the environment secure from intrusions like the phone, pets, children or other distractions? Is a shower available so she can wash afterwards? Is the lighting soft and the music serene? Does she know what to expect, so there are no jarring surprises? Similar soul-searching should be done when setting up any special pleasure scenario, whether it's lovemaking, dining, listening to music or purely psychological pleasures like reading or creative thinking.

Most of the time, we take an unthinking attitude toward pleasure, and fail to plan and maximize the enjoyment opportunities available. We can't fully appreciate our enjoyment experiences when pain enters the picture. Discomforts, intrusions, interruptions and annoyances are minor forms of pain which often can be avoided with some forethought. Pleasure seeking is indeed the normal, natural, spontaneous state of the psyche. As such, it should be treated with reverence and respect. Instead of the usual catch-as-catch-can approach, the wise bliss-seeker makes sure he plans in advance for his ecstasy adventures.

Pleasure pursuits should be approached almost like sacraments or spiritual experiences. Schedule pleasure sessions for yourself on a regular basis, and leave aside all cares and worries during these episodes. You'll soon find that thoughtful pleasure planning pays ample rewards. As a basic, primal urge, the pleasure drive demands direct, undivided attention. Frustrate it and you'll find yourself frus-

trated in return. Satisfy it and you'll be happier, more relaxed, contented and filled with plenty of energy to tackle other tasks. You'll be releasing power otherwise trapped from the suppression of your pleasure instincts.

Pleasure is not only natural and necessary, it's healthy. Some health-care professionals have described it as "therapy," and there's lots of wisdom in that view, especially in today's competitive world. Many of us spend most of our lives in self-denial, but in truth, we not only deserve pampering and pleasure, we need it for optimum well-being. It clearly is a wonderful means of self-expression, self-fulfillment and self-renewal. The pursuit of pleasure should certainly be among life's top priorities!

2

Peak Experiences and Self-Actualization

A key aspect of the psychology of pleasure is the notion of "peak experiences." This idea, part of the mainstream of modern humanist psychology, was pioneered by Dr. Abraham Maslow in his seminal study, *Toward a Psychology of Being.* Unlike Freud, who studied troubled, neurotic patients, Maslow focused on healthy, functioning people to find out what they had in common. His research on "self-actualizers"—his term for psychologically fit persons—enabled him to construct a "psychology of well-being," as opposed to Freud's "psychology of sickness."

Freud's model, as we saw in chapter one, portrayed the unconscious portion of the mind, the "id," as irrational, impulsive, harmful and something that needed tight social restraints. But what else could Freud construe, considering the fact that all his patients were highly neurotic? Maslow, in sharp contrast, believed that human instincts are basically benign, but that *repressing* them led to poor mental health and social disfunctioning. Maslow's pioneering work with top achievers, creative talents, leaders, dynamic performers and other "together" individuals showed him that when people are allowed to express their deepest selves and emotions, they are not destructive, but highly constructive.

Maslow erected a hierarchy of needs, each of which must be satisfied before moving on to the next stage. These basic needs are life, safety, security, belongingness, affection, respect, self-respect and self-actualization. As can be seen, many of these needs relate directly or indirectly to the drive for pleasure and pain avoidance. The first three needs, life, safety and security, are preconditions for all pleasure. Any threat to these needs makes pleasure impossible. The four higher needs can be seen as different aspects of the pleasure experience. Belongingness to a group, cause, ideology, etc., gives you a sense of purpose and security. Affection, including love in all its forms, is one of the central modes of pleasure enhancement. The respect of others is crucial for psychological health, as is self-respect. Only when one fully feels that one's goals and aims are accepted and respected—by both oneself and others—can one move forward in life.

As Maslow puts it, these basic needs must be fulfilled before one can reach one's full inner potential, the state of self-actualization. When social forces cut off the expression of these needs, the individual becomes stunted, stuck, unable to grow, as though he'd been locked in a vise. From our perspective, frustration of these fundamental needs also stunts one's pleasure capacity. The highest states of bliss can only be enjoyed when one possesses a sound psychological and physical structure. With key needs unmet, the pleasure drive may be channeled into unhealthy and even self-destructive expression. Drug addiction, alcoholism and compulsive eating and smoking are all examples of "pseudopleasures," substitutes for real pleasure when one finds essential desires are thwarted or repressed.

Maslow's highest need, when all the others have been met, is self-actualization. This refers to the full realization of one's potential, although it's not a static state, but a continual process of growth throughout life. Maslow found that self-actualizers (SAers) describe their experiences in terms that are remarkably similar to mystical and creative experiences. The themes of truth, goodness and beauty are all highly correlated in the SAer's life. One particularly significant experience that SAers continually seek is the "peak experience." Maslow describes these as "moments of highest happiness and fulfillment" and includes love, "the parental experience, the aesthetic perception, the creative moment, the therapeutic or intellectual insight, the orgasmic experience, certain forms of athletic fulfillment, etc." (Abraham Maslow, *Toward a Psychology of Being,* New York: Van Nostrand, 1968). During peak experiences, the individual feels himself to be "at the peak of his powers, using all his capacities to their best and fullest."

While all people occasionally have peak experiences, SAers have them more frequently and intensely. In some cases, the quest for peak experiences can become the focal point of an SAer's life. They make existence more meaningful, lend it added richness and impact and provide a vivid, intense sensation of *aliveness.* In most respects, peak experiences represent the ultimate pleasure pursuit. The pleasure philosopher or bliss-seeker—terms we'll discuss more fully in later chapters—has, as a central goal, the pursuit of pleasure in all areas of life, including work, love, sex and sensuality. But he also aims at *ultimate* or *total* pleasures at appropriate moments, and at those times he is certainly seeking peak experiences.

Since peak experiences are closely aligned with top pleasure pursuits, achieving them will be of central interest to anyone looking to enrich his existence. And since they are enjoyed most frequently and fully by SAers, pleasure advocates will also be interested in achieving the state of self-actualization. This involves releasing repressed desires and needs till the individual attains full expression.

One of the keys is self-awareness: knowing the forces that are at work both inside and outside yourself. In ensuing chapters, we'll be closely examining important pleasure prohibitions, taboos and engrained attitudes which interfere with ultimate enjoyment. We'll describe methods drawn from psychological, sociological and spiritual traditions for releasing oneself from such cultural restrictions. We'll distinguish between self-destructive pseudopleasures which compensate for unmet needs and true pleasures which directly satisfy such needs. But perhaps the key contribution this book will make toward self-actualization will be the introduction and teaching of pleasure techniques for use in all walks of life. Many therapists now realize that healthy pleasure is therapy in and of itself.

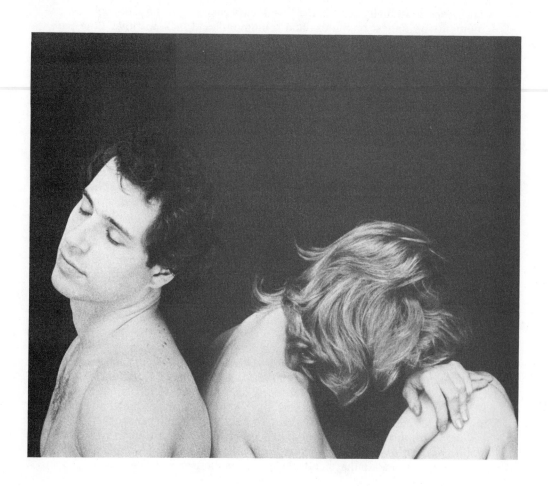

3

Pleasure Prohibitions

One of the most pervasive restrictions on man's pleasure drive is a series of cultural restraints which I call "pleasure prohibitions." Many of them can be traced to the dawn of civilization, while others are more recent products of religious and social movements only a few centuries old. A number of the restrictions made sense when they were initiated, as it was necessary to limit primitive man's raw instincts. But now, most are outmoded and obsolete. Still, they linger on, continuing to constrict and constrain enjoyment and self-expression.

One of the granddaddies of all is the sexual prohibition I refer to as the "erotic inhibition." As Freud correctly pointed out, control of the sex drive has been one of the hallmarks of civilization. This certainly made a lot of sense at the start, as promiscuous, random sexuality made it difficult to determine who had fathered whom. Channeling sex into monogamy and marriage made family life a much more viable possibility. At least the father could now be identified with some certitude. Family life in turn made possible social organization. Unfortunately, erotic inhibitions, now in force, result in overkill. Scriptural sources reflect this, as they predict dire consequences for masturbation, homosexuality, sodomy, etc.

But the sexual instinct is potent and irrepressible. The Bible contains passage after passage illustrating people's lapses, which continued unabated despite the threat of divine punishment. The sex drive is simply too expressive to be restricted to intercourse for the sole purpose of procreation. People continued to find other outlets, but the price paid was often a crippling sense of guilt. The consequences for "unlawful" sex included fears of the fires of hell, or the fires of men for accusations of heresy, devil worship or witchcraft. These fears were greatly enhanced during the later era of the Protestant Reformation, when Calvinist and Puritan doctrines depicted *any* bodily enjoyment as the route to eternal damnation.

During those times, the body was referred to as "mud" (St. Francis called it "Brother Ass," alluding to its low nature) and all things physical were considered barriers to spiritual development. The proper approach to the body was denial and asceticism, so it might be "purged" to the point where God approved. Even actions as innocent as regular bathing were suspect, because they might betray "sinful" concern for the body.

An outgrowth of these erotic inhibitions was another set of prohibitions called the "touch taboos." These extended the ban on sexual expression to sensuality

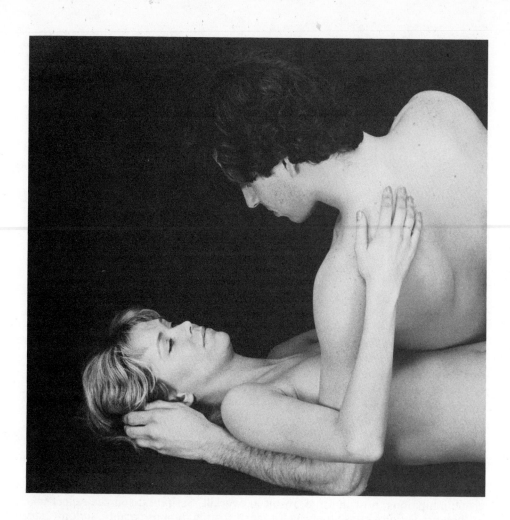

and touching. Nudity was forbidden, as was all bodily contact, whether alone or with others. The Puritans, for example, wore bulky, uncomfortable garb not only to hide the body, but to make it difficult to touch. Skin contact during sexual intercourse was to be severely limited, with suggestions made that slits for the genitals be sewn so sex could be consummated fully clothed. Virtually anything connected with the body was viewed as low, base and vile, a tool for the temptations of Satan.

Over time, the touch taboo spread in many different directions, and its modern version is widespread and multifaceted. Strangers are off limits for touching, as are people of the same sex. The elderly are rarely stroked. Family touching is circumscribed to a light peck on the cheek and superficial hug, and even then, only with family members of the opposite sex. Father-son touching has been nearly banned. About the only uninhibited stroking allowed in Protestant countries like the United States is with infants and pets. The restraints are relaxed, here, because no sexual threats exist.

However, as soon as children reach a certain age, the touch "spigot" runs dry in most American households. As the youngster matures, the touching begins to take on sexual connotations and the adults cut it off. The fact is, there is really no clear distinction between erotic inhibitions and touch taboos. In the Protestant tradition, touch and sex are clearly part of the same continuum, even though modern research reveals them as separate drives. This erotic/touch confusion causes most touch-oriented products and services to be seen as thinly disguised sex aids by unsophisticated thinkers. Thus, professional masseurs and masseuses are often viewed as prostitutes ("massage parlors"), even if highly trained and state-licensed. This Puritanical attitude also influences advertising policies. Most sensual products downplay their sexual significance.

For example, the manufacturers of mechanical massagers market their products in packages featuring smiling models using them on their faces, shoulders, or other "safe" areas. The sales pitch is generally geared to the health or hygienic benefits. The instructions innocently describe the clitoral-stimulator attachment as a "spot stimulator." One has to wonder what other spot this knob-shaped device could be used for. Other pleasure products use a similar advertising approach. The ads for shower-massage items focus as much on the cleansing benefits as on the more obvious enjoyment functions.

The fact is that pure, undisguised pleasure is still seen as sinful in the American mind. There's no problem if pleasure is hidden in some socially acceptable guise, like health. It's also okay if it's in some way connected to the work ethic, another area related to age-old pleasure prohibitions. Americans do allow themselves to "bust loose" after some outstanding achievement. Witness, for example, the wild champagne celebrations following sports-championship triumphs. In these circumstances, both the athletes and their rooters have license to put aside the work ethic and party on into the night. After all, when you reach the top of the heap, you surely deserve a break from the daily grind!

However, only one team and its supporters can be number one, and next season the grind begins anew. Meanwhile, the nonwinners wait until next year. None of the other rivals have cause to celebrate, not even the final runner-up to the champ. Instead of being proud of how far they've gotten, the World Series and Super Bowl runners-up usually feel inadequate. The "success is everything" work ethic

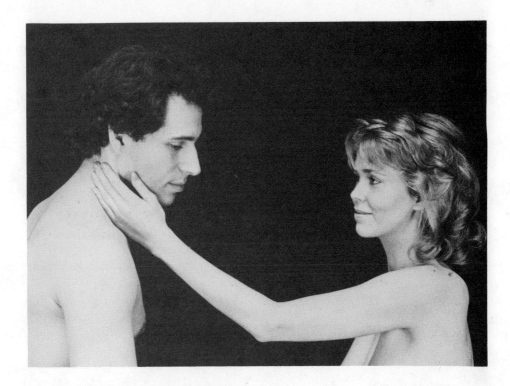

causes countless numbers of people in all walks of life to punish themselves until they finally make it to the top. Most never come close, and lead lives of quiet desperation. Those who do make it big frequently find that their lifestyle of self-abnegation leaves them unable to enjoy the spoils of victory. How often do we hear of the business tycoon who builds an empire, retires to enjoy it, then soon drops dead of stress-related disorders.

Our social norms, products of the pleasure prohibitions, clearly foster obsessive workaholism. Commercials feature mid-level managers working into the wee hours of the morning and overnight package-delivery services use ads that constantly bombard us with reminders of the frenzied pace of modern business. Our fears of "not making it" and "being left behind" are continually being reinforced.

Closely related to the work ethic is the "delayed-gratification syndrome" so common in the middle classes. Children are taught to put off their needs and desires until some future time. This begins with toilet training, then scheduled meals, and continues in other forms throughout life. We're told not to marry too young, not to spend money on things we enjoy, not to leave school early, etc. This advice makes sense to a point, but like all pleasure prohibitions, it turns into overkill. Learning to continually delay gratification until the "appropriate time" makes it awfully hard to relax and enjoy oneself when the time is finally right. Most of us are simply not designed to function on cue. The obsessive workaholic almost never finds the right time to let his hair down, at least not until age or infirmity makes it impossible to really enjoy himself fully.

The delayed-gratification syndrome limits the potential of most people. They get caught up in planning for the future and lose all spontaneity and sense of wonder. They stroll through a beautiful park and miss the plants because they're obsessed with some task at hand. They may plan all year for an ideal vacation, only to be bored and uncomfortable when it finally comes. They never live fully in

the now, but in the future, which never seems to arrive. They reach one goal, but instead of savoring the achievement, they're off and running toward another distant horizon. Constantly postponing our basic needs can lead to sexual disfunctions, constipation, insomnia, disturbed eating and other ills.

The healthy individual should strive for *balance* in his life, balance between work and pleasure, peak efforts and enjoyment. Pleasure and success are by no means at odds, but are actually well matched. Pleasure pursuits give you renewed vigor to help tackle your work tasks. It's the person who never takes a break, who never indulges himself, who never takes time for wild celebrations, that's the candidate for severe burnout. Pleasure pursuits like recreation, erotic play and massage help reduce stress, the number-one killer on the road to success. There are many creative ways to integrate ecstasy and work together in one harmonious whole.

You can alternate pleasure and work experiences, perhaps using pleasure as a reward for peak efforts (taking care not to destroy spontaneity and fall into the compulsive delayed-gratification trap). A better idea is to integrate pleasure into your success efforts, by doing work you especially enjoy or by learning to love the work you do. Another idea is to schedule regular pleasure periods throughout the week, just as you plan your work. That way, you'll be sure to receive a proper pleasure quotient.

We all need to reassess our attitudes toward pleasure and uncover the hidden ways pleasure prohibitions inhibit us. Careful self-analysis will reveal the extent to which you're allowing an inhibition to restrict your full self-expression. Remember, pleasure is your natural birthright. Your biology was built for it, and it makes little sense to deny what God has given you. You deserve as much enjoyment as you can get, and don't let any person, social institution or cultural norm try to convince you otherwise.

4

The Pleasure Philosophy

The pleasure philosophy is a modern alternative to outmoded pleasure prohibitions. Instead of being uptight and restricted, you become open and expansive. The first step is to examine your attitudes. Are they allowing you to get the most out of life, or do they stifle your fullest self-expression? If you find pleasure prohibitions controlling your life, start acting in the opposite way from their dictates. Begin with small steps, then move to larger, more liberating actions. When your behavior starts shifting, your attitudes will follow suit.

Once you attain a reasonable degree of freedom from pleasure prohibitions, you'll be more receptive to the pleasure philosophy. This perspective involves viewing the world from a unique angle, an angle which allows you to be open to all pleasure opportunities. You start to see pleasure possibilities in everything you do, in places you go, with people you meet. You understand that bliss is one of the fountains of life: a major force for health and well-being. You fully realize that not only do you *deserve* pleasure, but you *require* it for full self-expression. You realize that being denied pleasure robs you of a basic right.

You come to see pleasure experiences as a form of healing. Pleasure renews, refreshes and invigorates you, so you start to pursue it with added gusto. You regularly schedule pleasure activities in your life, making sure no week passes without some joy time. You eventually view pleasure as a legitimate, effective way to enhance your appreciation of existence. Pursuing pleasure expands your consciousness, your creativity, self-awareness and self-expression. Instead of following a dull, lackluster lifestyle, you become attuned to every opportunity to add zest, joy and spark to your days. Over time, you develop the "enjoyment outlook," an attitude which opens you up to all sorts of enchanting experiences. This attitude allows you to boost your pleasure quotient to the fullest.

The enjoyment outlook goes hand in hand with the pleasure philosophy. You start to see things with a childlike sense of wonder. Things around you no longer appear rigid, inflexible and predictable. Instead, they seem exciting, adventuresome and mysterious. The enjoyment outlook makes you sensitive to various ways of adding ecstasy to your erotic involvements, and other areas. The pleasure philosopher always seeks new ways to deepen and enrich his sensual escapades. He becomes a "connoisseur of ecstasy," maximizing and extending all joyful moments.

As he carries out daily tasks, the pleasure philosopher is always on the lookout for different ways to achieve new pleasure experiences. When he reads the paper, he searches for enjoyment items. Are there activities reported that he'd like to check out? Places he'd like to visit? Foods he'd like to try? Books he'd like to read? Products worth investigating? Even if he uncovers something he can't investigate right now, he can always file items away for future reference. Similarly,

30

when he's wandering through a shopping district, he always has eyes for things which can be creatively incorporated into his joy time. He's instantly intrigued with all kinds of pleasure products, like hot tubs, water beds, body oils, etc.

His pleasure sensitivities will often make him quite popular with other people. By filling his life with beauty and comfort, he'll cause others to enjoy associating with him. They'll find his unique outlook intriguing, and will want to learn more about him. His lifestyle will challenge others, and make them aware of their own pleasure inhibitions. They'll realize that being around him will teach them to let go of their hang-ups and increase their enjoyment of life's bounties. Everyone appreciates someone who knows how to have a good time. This will be particularly true of members of the opposite sex.

The pleasure philosopher's lovers stand to gain the most from his enjoyment outlook. Since sensual ecstasy is a cornerstone of all pleasure pursuits, the philosopher will devote a great deal of attention to it. He will become a master of blissful rites and ceremonies. While he may not be affluent, he'll make sure his money is wisely invested in creating appealing sensual settings. He may procure elaborate ecstasy equipment like hot tubs, Jacuzzis or saunas; or much simpler items, such as mechanical massagers, water beds or shower massagers.

He may not be into gadgets at all, but prefer to express himself in the realm of sensual ideas. Most lovers limit their erotic creativity to a few standard postures. Some go a bit further, learning from one of the countless "57 varieties" Western sex handbooks. These manuals provide some useful tips on technique, but they are usually mechanical and unspirited. The true erotic connoisseur goes well beyond the sex manuals into new realms of sensual possibilities. He sees the body as a total sensual playground, a fertile field of unlimited erotic options. He'll explore the sensual arts of cuddling, tickling and Swedish massage. These forms of expression will open up new dimensions in his love life.

He may investigate and learn different forms of bodywork therapies like shiatsu, deep-tissue massage and reflexology. He'll travel far afield of Western sexual literature to Eastern practices such as Tantric yoga eroticism, Hindu and Moslem manuals. He may incorporate intriguing ideas and techniques from taboo areas such as dominance and submission, bondage and S&M. He may study many of these systems. Whatever path he pursues, his aim will always be the ultimate pleasure experience.

His lovers will be fascinated and impressed by his sexual sensitivities and sophistication. The pleasure philosopher usually achieves a reputation as an "artist of love," and deservedly so. Whether he puts emphasis upon pleasure gadgets or exotic practices, his creativity and insights will separate him from the common herd. As a master of ceremony and ritual, he'll likely get involved in fantasy and role-playing. He and his partner may play roles like Master and Slave, Harlot and John or White Knight and Princess. They might experiment with switching sexual roles, with the man playing woman and vice versa.

He may encourage his lovers to express and even act out their sexual fantasies. He'll willingly play the parts they assign him. The pleasure philosopher will receive ample reward in return for his sexual receptivity. By fulfilling his partners' hidden desires, they'll be more than willing to reciprocate. A thoroughly open and receptive sex partner will allow the philosopher to pursue his pleasure with total abandon. He could not ask for more in his wildest dreams!

Whatever ways he expresses his sexual creativity, the pleasure philosopher will always take care to create the most comfortable and pleasant setting possible. Apart from special pleasure gadgets he may employ, he'll always be sure to involve as many senses as he can in the erotic experience. His setting may include mirrors in the bedroom for sight stimulation, body oil for touch, incense for smell, fine wine for taste and good music for sound. He creates a romantic atmosphere. Remember, the enjoyment outlook seeks to maximize the bliss payoff in all respects. Lovemaking should not be viewed as an isolated sexual episode, but rather as a grand drama in which you merge with your partner in all respects—physically, emotionally, psychologically and spiritually. Everything that surrounds you should be used as a prop for this magnificent erotic opera.

Therefore, make an extra effort to create a special romantic mood. Before making love, share some delicious snacks and fine wine or champagne (a nonalcoholic substitute is sparkling cider). But, be careful not to go too heavy on these. You don't want to feel too full, tired or lazy. Have just enough food and drink to spark the palate, excite the senses in anticipation of greater ecstasy. You may also consider sharing a shower or bath, and luxuriate in cleaning each other and toweling each other dry.

After your sex play, you should always continue the romance. Try cuddling, massaging, showering together, hot-tubbing, or any other creative afterplay. You should never just roll over and sleep, as that spoils the magical air you've worked so hard to create. You can also end your sensual involvement by returning for more snacks or drinks. Your experience will have been a total love ceremony, with a ritual beginning, middle and end. Your partner's expectations will be surpassed, and you can safely bet that he or she will be back for more. This thoughtful, thorough approach to pleasure pursuits is by no means limited to lovemaking. The practical pleasure philosopher always makes it his business to extract the most bliss possible from all his enjoyments, to execute unique "pleasure scripts" in all walks of life.

5

Mental Pleasure

We've mentioned how the brain produces its own pleasure chemicals, the endorphins, during periods of strenuous activity, stress or other heavy stimulation. We've seen how other physiological effects trigger pleasure sensations in the brain. Virtually all sensory input produces hormones which ultimately affect the brain. For example, lovemaking induces hormonal surges which course throughout the body system. Orgasm, the ultimate sexual sensation, results in a pronounced mental effect, quieting the mind and relaxing the entire body. Some esoteric schools consider orgasm to be an "altered state of consciousness" resembling meditation. Tantric yoga traditions teach that orgasm literally sends you to "seventh heaven" by surging a wave of psychic energy from the lower centers of the body to the top of the head, which is considered the connection between the material and spiritual realms.

It's easy to understand the biochemical pleasure effects on the brain caused by intense sensory stimulation. But it's not quite so simple to realize that *all pleasure really begins and ends in the mind.* In many respects, awareness is the seat of all enjoyment, as our interpretations deeply affect whether we perceive something as pleasurable or not. It's not so much the external phenomenon that counts, but our reaction to it. The same stimulus can cause markedly different responses, depending upon the values and conditioning of the individual. For example, the presence of a handsome, charismatic member of the opposite sex will usually produce pleasurable sensations in the average individual. But this may not be so if the viewer were exclusively gay, or brought up to see sex as "filthy" or "sinful." As the saying goes, different strokes for different folks.

In many respects, pleasure is intimately entwined with your mental attitude. A "bad attitude" toward life will color all your experiences in a negative fashion. Consider the different ways you get up in the morning. If you wake up with a grumpy, grumbly, uptight attitude, you've really gotten up "on the wrong side of the bed." With this start, it'll be awfully hard for you to milk any pleasure out of the day's events. You'll probably spend the rest of your day griping about the weather, traffic, work, the people you meet, etc. Even if you have the most spellbinding date set up that evening, you're not likely to approach it with full gusto. A negative viewpoint can cloud the most positive situations.

Contrast this with the individual who buoyantly bounces out of bed, sings in the shower and is bright and alive for the day's adventures. This person will ignore minor irritations, get along grandly with coworkers, do his job cheerfully and go home with a highly positive mindset. Whatever his evening activities, they're likely to be enjoyable and pleasant. Whether he winds up watching TV, reading the paper or making love to a special friend, his upbeat attitude will assure him of achieving the maximum pleasure quotient. It's worth repeating: Pleasure is a state of mind.

But how do you go about building a positive attitude, especially with today's constant bombardment of depressing news? One concrete step that can be taken is to avoid such news before going to bed. Don't watch the late evening news or read the paper right before sleep. The news is unavoidably slanted toward violent and sensational events, because they capture attention. You want to avoid such negative stimulation before slumber. Your subconscious mind is highly suggestible right before sleep, so injecting thoughts of violence and horror is the wrong way to lapse into dreamland.

And just as you want to avoid feeding your mind unpleasant images, you should cut down or eliminate snacking before sleep. Meals before bedtime force the blood to your stomach, when it's most needed in the brain. They can also cause nightmares and interrupt sleep with constant trips to the bathroom. Moreover, most late meals will be stored in your body as fat, since you have no way of working off the calories while asleep. You'll wake up sluggish and drained, the precise preconditions for that "bad attitude" that'll dampen your day's pleasure potential.

But there's more to a bad attitude that just your bedtime habits. Negative orientations toward life are often drummed into you from many directions, including family, schooling, church and other institutions. From the earliest years, people are constantly given messages which build a negative self-image. We're taught that we're noisy, messy, sinful, evil, naughty, disobedient, etc. We're rewarded for slavish, unquestioning conformity and sometimes punished for our expressions of individuality. This conditioning continues from the home to our educational systems to the work world. Add this conditioning to the daily diet of news concerning war, violence, crime, pollution, etc., and its hard for *anyone* to keep a positive outlook.

What's crucially needed is a way to counteract this negative bombardment. This is where "positive thinking" and its spinoffs come in handy. Positive thinking, psychocybernetics, Silva Mind Control and similar philosophies involve programming the mind with positive input to improve self-image. Some common techniques here include affirmations, visualization and inspiration. Affirmations are positive statements about what you'd like to be, do, or have. You set up a goal, then word it in the present tense as though it were a current reality. Examples: "I weigh 150 pounds and have a trim, 32-inch waist"; "I enjoy driving my new Mercedes-Benz"; "I love this beautiful vacation resort I'm visiting." You repeat these statements over and over before sleeping and after waking, when the mind is most receptive. You can write them on cards or tape record them. Don't get hung up on the "truth" of the affirmations. The idea is to plant positive seeds in your subconscious. This will affect your basic attitudes, and help guide you to the very success you seek.

Affirmations can be accompanied by visualization, in which you imagine yourself being, doing and having the things you want. Before bed and after waking, when the subconscious is active, spend a short time seeing in your mind's eye your ideal self, your desired relationships, job, possessions or whatever you seek. Positive self-image psychology holds that you gradually become what you envision yourself to be, and achieve what you imagine yourself achieving. You can reinforce affirmations and visualization through printed statements of your goals placed in strategic spots. You can carry typed affirmation cards in your wallet, or put them near your mirrors, or on the refrigerator, etc. The idea is to see them as often as possible so as to reinforce the message. Posters with positive messages can serve a similar purpose. Next to my shaving mirror, there's a small poster of a rooster crowing at the rising sun, with the message "Wake Up to a Bright New Day." This can help snap me out of any dreary wake-up mood. One warning, though: Don't let your affirmations be known to doubters and negative thinkers, especially those you live with. They won't understand what you're doing, and may ridicule your efforts to change and grow.

Inspiration works hand in hand with affirmations and visualization. Inspiration can come from books, magazines, motivational cassettes, speeches, workshops, etc. I recommend books like *The Magic of Believing* and *The Magic of Thinking Big,* magazines like *Success, Venture* and *Entrepreneur,* and tapes put out by organizations like Success Motivation Institute and Nightingale-Conant Corp. (see bibliography for a fuller list). Books and articles on the lives of great people can also be helpful, as can self-help workshops and trainings in the areas of leadership, motivation and achievement. Inspiration can also be derived from religious and spiritual activities.

In my own life, I find motivational and inspirational tapes to be particularly helpful. Upon rising, I put on a tape immediately, and continue listening throughout my morning meditation and workout, and on into the shower. I listen to each cassette for seven consecutive days, but on day six I sit down and listen carefully, taking notes on the messages. This way, I engage my conscious mind in a manner not possible during casual listening. On day seven, the message has been absorbed both consciously and subconsciously. You can also profitably listen to such tapes

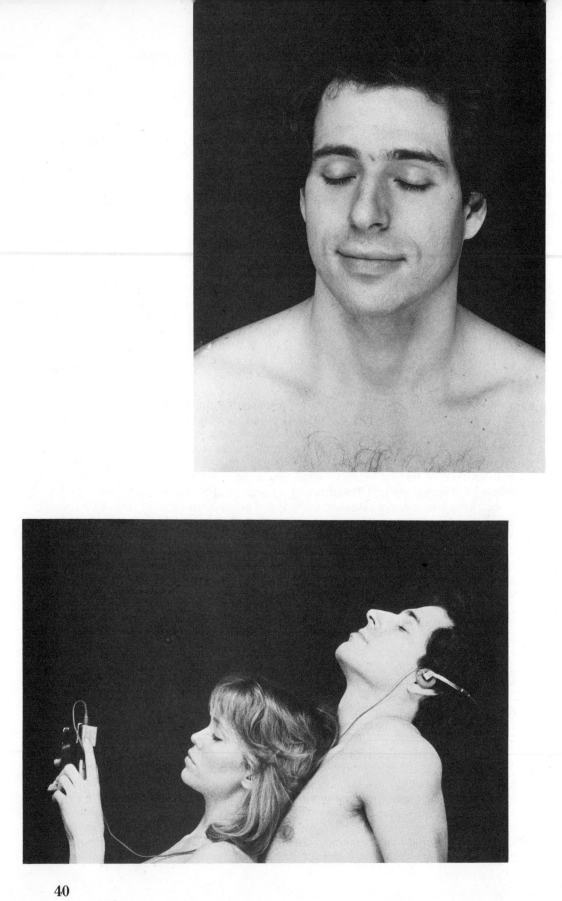

while driving, housecleaning, exercising or even while jogging with a Walkman-type mini-cassette player. Listening daily to a tape for one week will practically inscribe the message in your memory. Over time, you can reap tremendous benefits in knowledge, motivation and improved self-image.

These positive aids will eventually counteract any negative conditioning from the environment. You'll be calmer, more self-assured, secure and confident. You'll find yourself thinking, talking and acting more positively. The example you set will motivate others, and increase your popularity dramatically. Perhaps most importantly, your positive attitude will boost your pleasure quotient. Obstacles will be seen as opportunities, disappointments will become less significant and you'll start to see sunshine where formerly there was gloom. You'll literally "put on a happy face," making all your experiences more uplifting and enjoyable.

Another key aspect of mental pleasure is self-awareness. In general terms, this means "expanding your consciousness" to include ever-increasing amounts of knowledge, wisdom and alertness. This doesn't require becoming a bookworm or ponderous scholar, but it does entail an openness to new experiences, which few people care to cultivate. Unfortunately, most of us live our lives with blinkers on, limiting our interests to a few central areas, and ignoring everything else. Commonly, people are keenly aware of their immediate concerns like family, friends, work and perhaps local events, but little else. This is easily illustrated in mass-transit situations. On subways, railroads, buses, etc., people brush through the paper, skim magazines, glance at dime-store or romance novels, or just stare blankly into space.

In contrast, the pleasure philosopher gets *involved* with larger issues and uses his "downtime" wisely. He's the one likely to *read* (not skim) the news, and you may even find him with pen in hand jotting marginal notes down in serious, engrossing books. He may marvel at the passing sights, study other people's actions and expressions or do some thoughtful mental planning for the future. He might meditate, or silently repeat positive affirmations or do creative visualization. The pleasure philosopher understands that all life is interconnected, and wants to taste deeply of it *all,* not just a few morsels. The more he knows, the more aware he is, and the more he can manipulate his world to create maximum pleasure experiences. How can he appreciate, for example, whether water beds, hot tubs or Jacuzzis will increase his personal ecstasy if he tritely dismisses them as "kooky" or "kinky."

Instead, he'll make the effort to learn about areas he doesn't understand to see if they fit into his pleasure-schema. This is where the value of reading as a tool of self-awareness lies. The wonderful world of literature allows you to research any area at a leisurely, self-set pace, without taking the full plunge. Are you interested in building cabinets, but don't know where to start? Pick up a short book on the subject and find out if it's for you. You may discover the topic doesn't suit you, or you could find valuable leads to new modes of expression. The book might motivate you to try your hand at something else, or enroll in a course or program of study. Unfortunately, conventional education turns off most people to reading and organized learning. Education usually fosters a rat-race mindset in which the only worthy goal is grades, graduation and a degree. True learning is lost in the process. Curriculum requirements and exams lead to a distaste for learning. As you're forced to study, your natural curiosity becomes dulled and suppressed.

The spontaneous desire to explore and understand must be rekindled for maximum mind-expansion. Edmond Szekely, in his books *Our Eternal Companions* and *The Art of Study,* clearly illustrates the beauty of reading, learning and playing with ideas. The excitement of new discoveries, sharing the reflections of great minds, acquiring new skills, juggling new concepts: all these are part of the pleasure of reading and study. This continued expansion also defeats the tendency to lapse into negative thinking. For example, the negative thinker is constantly entrapped by self-imposed limitations. He tries his hand at sailing, for instance, doesn't do so well the first time and resigns himself to defeat with a cowardly, "well, I guess I just can't hack this." The lifelong learner, however, knows that he can lick nearly any problem through careful study and practice. His initial flops don't defeat him, but spur him on to greater effort.

Continual learning will also make you more interesting and attractive to others, thereby enhancing your pleasure possibilities. You'll never be at a loss for good conversation at parties and other social gatherings. People will come to you for information and clarification, and will admire your mental discipline and dedication. And learning need not be limited to books and the printed word. You can increase your skills and awareness by practicing the arts, hobbies, travel, sports and social involvements. You may learn a lot more about yourself by volunteer social-service work than by laboring over academic texts on psychology.

Over time, an organized program of acquiring new skills and knowledge will broaden your outlook and make you conversant in widely divergent areas. You'll come to appreciate the vast interconnections between all aspects of existence. Life will never be boring to you. As you stroll through a park and stop to inspect a flower, you'll see it from ever-shifting perspectives. You'll appreciate the biological view of the botanist, the aesthetic view of the poet, the transcendent view of the metaphysician and the naturistic view of the bee. They'll all seem beautiful and appropriate in their own contexts, as each is a shifting, kaleidoscopic glimpse of the unity of life. You'll break the bonds of cultural conditioning and see yourself as a multifaceted wonder of nature with chemical, biological, psychological, spiritual and other dimensions; always growing, always improving, always learning, no longer limited to narrow pockets of attention which constrict the vision of so many others. When you reach that high level of awareness, almost everything you perceive will be a source of pleasure.

Mind expansion, of course, is not limited to study and acquiring new skills. As we've seen, building a positive attitude is important in this endeavor, but mental pleasure can be gained in many other ways, including meditation, spiritual practices, exercise, sexual expression and drugs. We'll explore these areas in subsequent chapters.

43

6

Work

Social pleasure involves maximizing one's enjoyment in all phases of involvement with others. One crucial phase of social interaction is work, whether it entails self-employment or, more commonly, work for others. In either case, work almost always requires intense contact with other people, usually not of one's choosing. The merchant does not pick his customers, the salesman his prospects, or the writer his readers. And unless you are fortunate enough to be financially independent, work in one form or another cannot be avoided. Even the wealthy engage in activities entailing intense effort, whether they be politics, philanthropy, religion, social service or athletics. Being idle around the clock would be a total bore; we're simply not intended for complete nonproductivity.

Therefore, work is a reality which must be faced, and how we fare in that field will have a lot to do with our other pleasure pursuits. Work cannot easily be shunted off to one side, endured, as it were, with pleasure limited to so-called leisure time. We are not automatons which can be shifted from one mode to another at the flip of a switch. Our labors will intimately affect our other enjoyments. Only the schizoid or split personality would attempt to clock in eight hours of drudgery and the rest of his waking time in ecstasy. Yet this is very much what many of our social myths try to enforce.

Early on, we're taught that we have to work in order to survive. Parents, school, church and other institutions drum this message in until it's no longer questioned. We soon learn that work is the opposite of play and having a good time. Children see parents trudging in from work at night, exhausted, uninspired, downcast, ready for an evening of martinis and TV. The educational system amply reinforces this model: We are taught to unquestioningly conform, be docile, obedient, cut corners when we can. Education becomes an endurance contest to collect that diploma, degree or certificate—not a place to excel. In all too many work settings, people become experts at "killing time"—paper shuffling, feigning busyness, doing just enough to get by—the same traits nurtured in school.

The fact is, work does not have to be a bore. Once again, much depends upon one's attitude. "As a man thinketh, so is he," says the psalmist, and that's particularly true in this context. You can be doing the most creative, interesting work in the world, but if you buy the outmoded, conventional attitudes towards employment, you too will come home drained and dragged out. On the other hand, a beaming, optimistic personality can get you through the most boring task with a smile and a sense of purpose and accomplishment.

The first stereotype that must be broken is the "have to" sentiment about work. No matter how many cultural messages bombard you about how you must "work to live," you *do* have a choice in the matter. Some people are not cut out for the nine-to-five grind, no matter how much they steep themselves in Protestant-ethic ideology. We all have inner cycles, including the twenty-four hour circadian

rhythm which determines our optimum sleep and waking periods. Take someone who functions at peak form at 4:00 A.M., force him into a nine-to-five nook, and you have a square peg in a round hole.

A viable alternative may be further education. Some people give the job market a crack, don't like what's available and decide to upgrade their skills. Getting a new degree or certificate or license can be rewarding, but there's no guarantee that you'll land a new job once you graduate. And even if you do, you may not like it any more than the old one. Perhaps worst of all, education has become prohibitively expensive. Loans and grants have dried up, tuition has soared, and you still have to pay for living expenses.

A better alternative is to maintain a simple, modest lifestyle, at least until you're undeniably solvent enough to afford luxuries. This allows you a wide latitude of choice. Too many people lock themselves into a maze of mortgages, car payments, childcare expenses, etc., to be able to get by on a reduced income. A typical pattern is for someone to graduate from college, get a good-paying position, then immediately become overburdened with expensive installment credit purchases. In the working and middle classes, men often marry quite young, and get wrapped up in the "Great American Dream" of the suburban home, two-car garage, two kids, etc. In short order, an individual like this starts straining his budget to the limit, just barely making it from month to month in a frantic effort to "keep up with the Joneses." Then the economy sours and he's left with a few hundred a month in jobless benefits to cover a $3,000-plus-per-month lifestyle. He has no option then but to pursue another high-paying job, because he's become a victim of the vicious pattern of "conspicuous consumption."

A newer version of this self-imposed prison is the "swinging singles" lifestyle. Here, the young worker gets a decent job and decides to taste the "good life." Problem is, the good life usually involves the same mindless overspending. A well-paid executive secretary may easily blow a five-figure salary on frivolous clothes, frequent dining out, expensive jewelry and other frills. A male financial analyst commanding six figures may follow the same road, burning his cash on fast cars, "big-time spending," a designer wardrobe, etc. These people are literally on a treadmill, with little freedom to act or shift gears. While there's nothing intrinsically wrong with material goods—all bliss-seekers use and enjoy them—compulsive, conspicuous consumption is closer to an addiction. Freedom of choice, action and movement are keystones of real pleasure, and a credit-card, hand-to-mouth lifestyle, doesn't afford much freedom.

The true pleasure philosopher does not take his cues from mass psychology, and couldn't care less about the Joneses. He knows that pleasure is a state of mind which does not depend on material wealth. Quality, not quantity, is what counts for him. In a later chapter, we'll look at pleasure products, some of which are quite lavish and costly. They can indeed be nice to own, but they're hardly necessary to produce ultimate pleasure experiences. A man and woman alone on a simple mattress with clean bedding can generate all the ecstasy one needs. Anything else is just icing on the cake.

I know many people who have built alternative lifestyles that keep them completely out of the nine-to-five work grind. Some live in collective or communal situations with others, thus reducing living expenses to a bare minimum. Others use manual skills to rebuild old houses, lofts or apartments which they can then live in quite cheaply. Still others share inexpensive living quarters with a single roommate or lover, splitting costs. In most cases, people like these specialize in alternative forms of employment. They may work part-time, or on a temporary basis, working just enough to afford their simple lifestyles. Entrepreneurial types may run small-scale businesses, like selling handmade crafts. In many cases, these same people are using their extra time to learn and practice skills that will one day pay big dividends. That young woman waiting tables may be an aspiring

actress, artist or musician. While she may seem "poor" now, she may set the world on fire in a few years.

The main lesson to be learned here is that you should resist cultural demands towards conspicuous consumption and mindless materialism until you're quite financially secure. Instead of burning the bucks you now make in the fast lane, put a good percentage of your earnings in solid investments, especially in your early working years. Then you'll have a cushion to fall back on in case of hard times. Don't be obsessed with the latest fashions, gadgets or gizmos, but follow your own prudent path. If your friends won't like you if you stop being a big spender, they're hardly the kind of company you need. And if freedom means more to you than money, consider an alternative work pattern outside the nine-to-five mainstream. Believe me, the pleasures of being lord over your own time pay tremendous dividends. While everyone else is locked up in their offices or factories, you can shop when you want in uncrowded stores, bank when you desire, travel at your whim, and work when *you* choose. If you can handle a bit of insecurity about regular paychecks, being your own boss is surely one of life's grandest joys.

But if nine-to-five labor is your cup of tea, there's no reason you still can't maximize your enjoyment. You can make the most out of any task—and that includes household chores as well as employment. The key once again is your attitude. You first must decide if the job is something you choose to do. As we've pointed out, there are no true "musts" in life. For example, you can always have the laundry sent out or hire someone for your domestic chores. And you can always quit a job that's simply impossible to live with. Don't buy all that conventional garbage about having to have a "perfect résumé" with no gaps in employment at all. This is a complete myth. There are scant few people who haven't quit or been fired at some time, especially with all the recent recessions. And you can always arrange a résumé so that gaps get covered up.

If a job just doesn't cut it with you, explore your alternatives, then give advance notice of your resignation. If you're really cooperative and gracious, the boss may permit you to train your successor, and give you a nice letter of recommendation. Ideally, you should not quit until you've lined up something new, so your job search should start well before you quit. But don't let conventional wisdom trap you here either: If a job is making you emotionally or physically overwrought, *just get out.* Your health is much more important than doing things according to the book.

If finances are a real obstacle, there are strategies for getting unemployment benefits. If your relationships with higher-ups are basically good, you may be able to work out a deal which includes both unemployment compensation, a clean company record and a reference note. Offering to stick around and train your successor is one bargaining chip in such a deal. Or a doctor can always affirm that job pressures and stress may be wearing you down, thus supporting a disability benefits claim. An excellent and effective tactic is to do fantastic work, then run a power play on your boss. Ask for more control, for a say in work policies, or a hand in management decisions. Be polite, civil and sensible, so you can't be denied unemployment compensation due to "misconduct." Most bosses are so irrationally addicted to control that you'll get your walking papers in no time. And with a faultless work record, a reference letter as well. While your boss may let you go because of an assertive personality, he'll empathize with your ambitions, appreciate your topflight performance, and be unlikely to blackball you.

But once you've found the right niche in the work world, there are plenty of things you can do to maximize your pleasure potential. The ultimate ideal, of course, is to be doing work you'd be glad to do without pay. Many athletes and creative artists do exactly that, blending work and play in a beautiful combination.

But there are still lots of options even if you're not so fortunate. For example, the strategy we just mentioned for being gracefully dismissed, working at maximum efficiency while pushing for more control. If you shift tactics just a bit by being less confrontative or demanding with your boss, you may just achieve the added control you seek. You can do this by working overtime without pay, volunteering for tough assignments, being eager to tackle new responsibilities.

One of the keys to job success is people management. In its simplest form, it means getting along with others, avoiding or mitigating conflict and getting others to help you in your given tasks. People management is relevant regardless of your position, but the rules do shift according to whether you're labor or management. When I edited *Creative Management* magazine, I was amazed at the wide variety of theories available about the art and science of handling others. There are myriad schools of thought, like "tough-minded management," "Japanese-style management," "humanistic management," etc. Many of these models are complex, convoluted and more suited to mathematics than mankind. What I'll try to do here is draw together some simple rules from these various sources.

If you are an "ordinary" employee, you must get along with both peers and management. Peer relations with other workers are not that different from the way you treat friends and acquaintances, with mutual respect, cooperation and responsibility. However, there are some crucial distinctions. Most importantly, corporate life inevitably involves some form of "gamesmanship," and you have to be on guard for it. Your fellow employees, while seemingly cordial, may harbor high, sometimes ruthless ambitions, and may be locked into vicious grapevines with branches all the way to the top. Therefore, it generally pays not to get too chummy with anyone on the job. Keep things amiable but casual, and avoid

company politics whenever possible. *Don't* reveal personal secrets, gossip about others or gripes about the company. No matter how good your work performance is, you'll soon be branded as a blabbermouth or troublemaker. It's also important not to become identified too closely with an office faction or clique because this may close you off from others. The best strategy is to let *everyone* think you like them and are sympathetic to their side. It's fine—in fact smart—to listen to gossip and "inside" information; just don't spread it around or take sides.

As for dealing with management, the same rules apply about getting too chummy and avoiding cliques. But dealing with higher-ups is a bit more complicated. You have to be a bit of an amateur psychologist and find out the basic needs, motives, goals and drives of your boss. What is his or her "personal style"? Cautious and conservative? Bold and daring? Driven and ambitious? Laid-back and lazy? Whatever it is, you'd do best to fit yourself into its pattern. You learn the boss's style by studying how he treats others, and how he does his own work. Your main role is to assist him in his efforts, even if you disagree with his means or ends. Portray yourself as a cooperative "team player" willing to go the extra mile. Be obedient without being spineless; don't argue, gripe or spread rumors. One of the worst mistakes, if you want to make it, is to be militant about your "rights" as an employee, for example by refusing to do things that fall outside the strict description of your job title. Your employer may not be able to force you to go out for coffee, but he or she can force you out of the job. And forget about federal suits, human rights complaints and the like. You may win battles like these for unfair treatment, but lose the war.

Remember, you *chose* to go the corporate route. If you don't like its rules and games, you can always get out and pursue other alternatives. But as long as you're there, you must play the game one way or another. By being cooperative and compliant, you may not get any great rewards, but at least you'll be making life easy for yourself. You'll be less likely to be threatened, targeted or harassed. You'll be paving a smooth road for yourself, which is a key to successful work life.

You come in, do your job, avoid struggles: a simple, easy course to follow. Don't forget, part of pursuing pleasure is avoiding pain, so make it your business not to be controversial, uncooperative or negative in any way.

The managerial role is even more complex. Unless you're at the very top of the ladder, you have to please higher-ups, cooperate with peers and motivate subordinates. The middle manager should act toward his boss in much the same manner that the worker handles his supervisor: be cooperative, compliant and uncontroversial, unless you harbor strong ambitions, in which case a bolder, more aggressive posture may serve better. With peer-level fellow managers, cooperation is critical. Try to override factions and politics with a "teamwork" approach: "We're all in this together, so we may as well unite and help each other out." One caution, though: Don't let any other manager get the idea he can dominate you and dump his work on you. Do your fair share and maybe a tad more, but don't let another manager rip you off. Firmly, but politely, tell him or her to handle his or her own load.

Managing subordinates may be your toughest challenge. Today's work force is better educated, has higher expectations and is quite zealous about its "rights." Antidiscrimination laws and sexual harassment statutes contribute to an "us against them" mindset. The average worker may be unmotivated, lazy and even outright antagonistic. Without surrendering your authority, you have to pierce the layers of resistance and learn the likes and dislikes of your workers. It's again a question of uncovering their personal styles. Observe how they handle work tasks, interact with others, etc. Pick up some good books on management psychology for more information (see bibliography). Eventually, you'll get a feeling about the strengths and weaknesses of your workers, and you can use that knowledge to allocate assignments. The bold, assertive type can be best utilized on tough, challenging projects, while the quiet, retiring sort may be best suited to dull, tedious tasks. It's a matter of making maximum use of the human resources available to you. If someone is totally unsuitable, there's always the option of dismissal, but this should never be done thoughtlessly and without full consideration of the possible consequences.

One key tip for managers is not to be so overbearing and tyrannical that you beat your underlings into meek lambs. Give them room to grow to full potential. Remember, no manager can do everything by himself; he must delegate responsibilities to others. If you break your workers' spirits by petty ego-flexing and power-tripping, you're robbing yourself of your chief resource: a dependable team. Only humans, not sheep, can carry out responsible actions. Be fair and reasonable with your subordinates and they'll likely treat you the same way.

And what does all this management psychology have to do with pleasure? Quite simply this: The better you get along with coworkers, the easier your job will be. The absence of conflict, political hassles and other irrelevant distractions will free up your time and allow you to concentrate on your work. The fewer obstacles, the better. And what if your work is boring, tedious, dead-end, uninspiring? Once again, we return to attitudes. Whatever task you face, on or off the job, should always be given your best shot. You can always balance a dull work life with an exciting nonwork life. But more importantly, you should endeavor to develop internal standards of excellence, a sense of pride and craftsmanship which will motivate you toward peak efforts all the time.

From this perspective, excellence can be its own reward. With this attitude, any task can be a source of pleasure. You know in your heart that you've given it your best, which leads to a great deal of internal peace and satisfaction. And when others find that they're not forced to trick or cajole you into doing a good job, the external rewards will follow as well.

7

Success and Achievement

Success and achievement are obviously closely connected with work, since most major accomplishments take place there. But they are by no means limited to work, and in fact far transcend it. The joy of success is a very special feeling, a triumphant euphoria which ranks among life's greatest pleasures. Remove accomplishment from one's life and pleasure often becomes limited to raw sensation seeking and mindless hedonism. A success-oriented lifestyle is not only a pleasure to pursue in and of itself, but provides the discipline and structure to enjoy other pleasures. Once again, balance is the key: here, the balance between dedicated achievement and having fun.

Naturally, success is relevant to all the topics covered in this book. One can be a success at love, work, friendship, spiritual development, etc. Success techniques for these subjects are treated in detail in their respective chapters. Here we want to focus on the joys of success itself, as well as the success lifestyle. America indeed is the land of success, and "making it," "moving on up" and "getting ahead" are all central social themes. But the success we're focusing on here is not merely external, worldly achievement, which can be and often is vulgar and trivial. In fact, we have to avoid the all-too-common American "success syndrome" in which all else is sacrificed to pursue some particular accomplishment. This often becomes an obsessive/compulsive neurosis in which making it becomes one's sole object of worship.

The compulsive success syndrome can render you superficial and empty in other areas of life. For example, corporate executives on the way up often neglect their families, leading to broken homes and delinquent kids. When they do reach the top, they may find themselves isolated, alone and alienated from others. Newspapers are filled with stories of people who toiled for years to achieve some objective, then dropped dead shortly after attaining it. This is also reflected in the high death rate among retirees—after leaving their field of endeavor, they have no drive left to live, no sense of purpose to continue on. What's perhaps even worse is the case in which someone's major goal is completely thwarted. In some situations, this leads to an even quicker demise. One recent example: the rapid death of Senator Hubert Humphrey after his final presidential nomination bid failed. He died of cancer, a disease many connect with a major emotional loss.

So it pays to keep a healthy perspective when it comes to success. Certainly, you should avoid nurturing one burning ambition to the exclusion of all else. Put your success eggs in a number of baskets, and don't become driven by any single accomplishment. If anything is more important than success, it's equanimity. Win or lose, the true success retains peace of mind at all times. As we pointed out in the chapter on work, it's not so much results that count but putting forth your best effort. When you give it your best shot, you've succeeded—no matter what the outcome. What we're aiming at here is to build the type of spirit you find in fine craftsmanship: the pride and general sense of well-being from a job well done. Authors, artists, leaders and athletes, among others, all understand this feeling.

There is usually a close connection between the inner sense of craftsmanship and external rewards. In *Getting Rich Your Own Way,* Dr. Srully Blotnick studied two hundred self-made millionaires and found some startling revelations. Unlike what conventional wisdom would predict, these achievers did not make it big by aiming at becoming millionaires, or by "hard work" or via good connections. Dr. Blotnick found that the money came about naturally as a by-product of their doing what they loved to do best. They enjoyed their work to the fullest—for some it was more like play—and continued to put forth peak efforts for the inner satisfaction gained from quality. And while they did not actively court big bucks, over time their excellence came to be recognized and their products and services were amply paid for.

Of course, none of these successful millionaires shunned the recognition and remuneration their quality work ultimately brought them. The merger of internal standards of excellence and outer rewards can be a potent combination. The quality performer—as opposed to the "big-bucks artist" only concerned with rewards—who makes it to the top truly enjoys one of the greatest pleasures of all. As long as you don't fall victim to the "success syndrome" we've discussed, ultimate achievement in some area can almost be an orgasmic experience. We've all seen the absolute joy and ecstasy of athletes winning world championships— the glory of Olympic victory, World Series triumph. These are top-level peak experiences, the total fulfillment of one's inner potential, one of the rarest forms of pleasure.

But such victories are hardly won overnight. Just as Dr. Blotnick's millionaires often labored for years without being acknowledged, all ultimate achievement is underpinned by long, dedicated discipline. While the spectator may vicariously share his moment of triumph, the top athlete may have spent years of dawn-to-dusk training all by himself. And so it is with all of life's big winners. Practice, practice, practice: there's the key. And while you may not seek fame or fortune, discipline is required for success in almost every endeavor, including the pursuit of pleasure. The pleasure philosopher, as we've indicated, is a connoisseur of ecstasy. He learns to pass up phony, inferior or pseudopleasures for the things that really count. Any guy, for instance, can grab some cheap thrills by going to a topless bar and guzzling drinks 'til he needs to be carried out. Contrast this low-level approach with planning an elaborate lovemaking scenario replete with fine wines, good food and a comfortable, nice setting.

The smart bliss-seeker aims to "succeed at pleasure" and he's willing to put the effort out to achieve high states of enjoyment. There are several techniques taken from business management which can be used to maximize accomplishment in any area, pleasure or otherwise. The first we've already discussed: setting your own personal standards of excellence and forgetting about those of the crowd. The second is "time management," which refers to the most effective use of time to pursue your ends. There are many excellent guides to the subject, especially Lakein's concise *How to Get Control of Your Time & Your Life.* Basically, time management shows you how you're using your time now so you can put it to better use.

For example, closely examine your time expenditures, hour by hour, for a week or two, using a chart. You'll probably be shocked at the results. Like many, you'll note large chunks of time literally thrown in the gutter on trivial, meaningless pursuits. Many people are stunned when they learn how much time they waste on meals, newspapers, TV, phone calls, etc. No wonder there's never enough time

for the truly important things in life! Another success technique closely aligned with time management is goal setting. After you've learned how you currently use your hours, the next step is to reallocate your time so you're working on key goals. But first you have to set them.

With pen and paper, sit down and figure out what you really want to accomplish in life. You can break down goals in terms of different subjects, like finances, work, relationships, etc. You should also divide them in terms of time: five-year goals, three-year goals, one-year, six-month, etc. Then you prioritize them. Top-level goals can be labeled "A," mid-level "B," lower-level "C," and the rest discarded for now. Then you'll have a list of specific goals arranged according to time, class and priority. This will guide your time-management aims. Generally, you want to make sure that you spend the most time on "A" goals, next on "B" and last on "C." But if an "A" goal is a real toughie or very long-range—like becoming chief executive at your company—be sure to allocate at least an hour a week to this. Even ten minutes a day can provide tremendous progress over time. You can whittle seemingly enormous tasks down to size by just chipping away at them daily, much like a little stream of water will erode solid boulders eventually. For example, by reading ten to twenty pages a day, I was able to complete the massive, 1,377-page *Scofield Reference Bible*—replete with tiny, elaborate footnotes—in a few short months. The same method can work to conquer any seemingly formidable undertaking. Just cut it down to small, manageable chunks and tackle one at a time.

Time management and goal setting can be aided by still another success technique borrowed from business: organization. Organization can be invaluable for both personal and professional efforts. Creating a filing system, putting your books and tapes in order, keeping clear records, cleaning out your closets, maintaining an uncluttered desk—all these are ways to get organized. While the process of putting your life in order may take some time and effort, it will be more than made up for later. Organization lets you locate valuable documents, tax receipts, correspondence, records, etc., with little hassle. It also gives you a nice sense of security, because you're really on top of things. You know where everything fits, how your system works and where to easily find whatever materials you need. An orderly system contributes to an orderly mind. A home computer with appropriate software can be a valuable aid in getting organized, because it drastically expands your recordkeeping and retrieval abilities.

Time management, goal setting and organization all work together to liberate you from wasted effort and help free you for what you really want to do. You can use the extra time gained to engage in enticing pleasure practices, or plow through to ultimate achievements or, even better, do both. Master these methods and you'll build an unstoppable achievement orientation into your life. That will allow plenty of deep drinks from the heady, ecstatic wine of success.

8

Friendship

True friendship is a precious experience which seems to be fading fast in our increasingly alienated, mechanized times. In most large cities, people seem to be spending more time developing "relationships" with personal computers, video games and check-cashing machines than with other people. Yet no machine will ever provide the warmth, love and pleasure of human companionship. Unfortunately, friendship seems to be becoming a lost art. People have come to view others more and more as objects, means to an end, rather than ends in themselves. "What's in it for me" and "what can I get from him" are all-too-prevalent attitudes these days.

The flip side of this is the tendency for people to always be on guard. Suspicion, mistrust and cynicism about others' motives are quite common. Simple, ordinary courtesies are often ignored in interpersonal dealings. Phone messages go unreturned, commitments are broken at whim, confidences violated, etc. The reasons for man's increasing inhumanity to man are probably linked to other recent social shifts. Increasing urbanization and the breakup of the extended family have resulted in more and more contact with strangers. In old-style agricultural settings and small towns, almost everyone knew, or was related to, everyone else. But in the modern city and suburb, the majority of people one meets are strangers and this can lead to devaluation of people in general. Today's high-tech orientation also contributes to depersonalization. As machines replace humans we learn to relate to everything mechanistically. Machines don't have desires or needs and we tend to view people in much the same fashion.

This technocratic approach to human relations is evident in the booming popularity of "self-help" and "how-to" books. Most of these manuals stress "techniques" for relating to others in the areas of sex, love, relationships, business, etc. It's almost as though we've forgotten the simplest human communication. And while these books may provide useful insights and advice, their approach treats people as objects. Learn the "57 varieties" of sex postures, for example, and you'll be a sure hit as a lover. This alienation is further emphasized by modern advertising. Ads depict people as a commodity to be marketed. Drive this car, use this toothpaste, wear these clothes, and you'll be sexier, more attractive and desirable. The unspoken message is that you're not okay just the way you are, but must be merchandized and repackaged according to Madison Avenue's dictates.

Ads not only undermine a healthy self-image, but they often depict others as pawns to be pushed around. For instance, mothers are shown controlling their families through food; men manage women with fancy cars and jewelry; women manipulate men through perfumes and sexy garb. Example after example can be cited of people being portrayed as mindless automatons to be programmed by some material reward. The sum total of the influences of urbanization, technoc-

racy and advertising is the depersonalization and dehumanization of our relation-ships. Is it any wonder people have lost the ability to appreciate true friendship?

And just what are the elements of genuine friendship? They include openness, vulnerability, humanity, and interest in the other as a *subject,* not an object. Friendship means true intimacy and empathy, not a superficial, skin-deep "hail fellow well met" involvement which lasts only as long as you're "getting some-thing out of it." Theologist Martin Buber has described it as an "I-Thou" relation-ship, referring to the deep communication and sense of unity characteristic of close friendships. Friends are committed to each other's welfare, and are literally willing to "give the shirt off their backs" to help out an ailing comrade. If this sounds hackneyed or clichéd, it's only because of the pervasive influence of modern commercialization and the "me generation" philosophy.

Friendship and pleasure are intimately entwined. We are thoroughly social ani-mals, and deeply need others to care for us in a real sense. We need to be nurtured and loved, not for some role or function we play, but for what we are *inside.* And while this may seem less obvious, we also need to care for and nurture others the same way. This is because we all retain parenting instincts, even if the social order tries to restrain them. When someone in the street is hurt or in trouble, we *feel* the pain, even if we've been indoctrinated to "keep away from strangers." We may ignore the person's plight, but it registers somewhere in our inner psyche. And it's this inner aspect of our being that craves friendship.

There's a thin line between friendship, sex and love, and in fact they often overlap. Friendship can be viewed as a more placid, steady form of love, not burning quite as hot, but still quite bright. While they are rarely found in the same relationship, friendship and sex can definitely coexist. You can be friends with a member of the opposite sex, and still enjoy each other's bodies. In fact, there's a good possibility that "sexy friendships"—to coin a phrase—may be increasingly prevalent in the future. Modern love relationships are characterized by chaos and confusion, with neither sex quite sure about the proper role to play. In this atmo-sphere, sexy friendships provide a looser, more flexible alternative than conven-tional commitments. Certainly, the choice between a sterile, nonsexual "platonic relationship" and a full-blown love affair is far too limited for today's sophis-ticated singles. Now that women are achieving full parity with men in all areas, it makes sense that novel forms of involvement would evolve, including the combi-nation of sex and friendship.

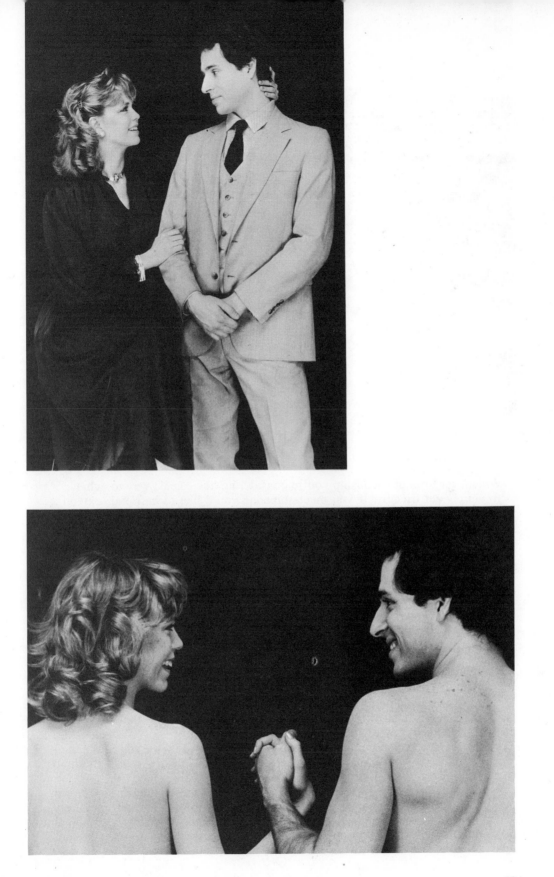

Whichever form of friendship you're considering, the easiest way to achieve it is to simply act friendly. If you meet someone you'd like to befriend, extend a welcome hand and show the person genuine warmth and compassion. Make him or her comfortable in your presence by being nonjudgmental, honest and sincere. Be prepared for the fact that the other individual may rarely have been exposed to real friendship, and may look upon your motives with suspicion. But, if you really want that person to be a part of your life, you'll have to take some risks to prove your good intentions. You might have to be patient and persistent if your initial overtures are met with resistance. For example, at first your new acquaintance may not return your calls, or could even pull a no-show on you on a planned date. You have to be philosophical about such lapses, remembering that most people have been indoctrinated in the dehumanized, objectivized mode of viewing others.

New people you meet may simply not understand the value of friendship like you do, so you may find yourself in the role of teacher—or, even worse, martyr—at times. You should be prepared for disheartening disappointments, but always give others the benefit of the doubt. Don't sell them short until they've proven beyond a doubt by their actions that they're incapable of reciprocal friendship. The process of removing phony social masks and facades may frighten the daylights out of some, and it may take some time for them to break out of the rigid roles fostered by mechanization, technology, and advertising.

People from the helping professions, or from humanistic, spiritual or consciousness-raising orientations are most likely to be receptive to you. Those from purely competitive, conventional and commercial backgrounds—especially a combination of these—are more likely to have worshiped extensively the idol of self-interest and are less likely to empathize with you.

But there are certainly no hard-and-fast rules in this area. You can be heartily befriended by the most hard-nosed business executive, or betrayed by the most idealistic humanist poet. Don't be discouraged by failures or frustrations in building friendships, because each attempt can be a valuable learning experience for the future. Just continue to be kind and considerate in your dealings, and you'll eventually gather a core group of close friends. And such comrades will definitely enhance your pleasure life. For one thing, they'll serve to insulate you from the crippling loneliness and isolation so characteristic of our troubled times. The pleasure philosopher enjoys being popular, because more close friends mean more party invitations, phone calls, companionship, conversation and opportunities for joint bliss seeking. An ideal situation is to have a variety of friends from widely differing backgrounds: this diversity will ward off boredom and apathy and help assure you of interesting, exciting experiences.

You don't need a large group to be a success at friendship. Even the most popular people have a small number of particularly intimate buddies, plus a wider circle of more superficial acquaintances. Some people have little use for the wide circle, and prefer to limit themselves to an inner core of intense soul brothers and sisters. These are particularly special relationships in which you lick each other's wounds, share each others sorrows, partake in each other's pleasures—the type of involvement you can freely turn to during disturbing moments of confusion, crises or despair. It takes only a few friends like these to fulfill your social instincts and provide a soothing peace of mind quite conducive to launching your most ambitious pleasure escapades.

9

Love

Above all else, the pleasure philosopher is a connoisseur of peak experiences. He deeply appreciates situations which grip him on an emotional, spiritual and physical level. Superficiality is usually not his cup of tea. He is a dedicated sensation seeker, and the more enticing the sensation, the better. Because of this, the pleasure philosopher tends to be an ideal lover. He drinks heartily at love's magical fountain, since he understands that love is one of the highest peak human experiences possible.

The purest pursuit of pleasure usually entails a fully developed romantic spirit. The pleasure philosopher seeks beauty in all places, and he cannot help but appreciate the wonder and splendor of shared love. He sees love as the central bond between people, the social glue that keeps them cemented emotionally. Without love, there'd be little reason for cooperation, empathy, caring, generosity and all the other civilized qualities of life. Love exists in myriad forms, and the bliss-seeker will look for it in all its manifestations, whether in the family, in friendship, with pets or with nature. But he's most apt to worship at the exalted throne of romantic involvement with a member of the opposite sex. Because this is where it all comes home: the primal human attachment, the experience immortalized by enraptured poets throughout eternity.

Unfortunately, there are certain barriers to the full expression of romantic love, and each pleasure pursuer should examine himself to see if he's fallen prey to them. I call these "love blocks" because they can usually be traced to early attitudes which interfere with full loving. Perhaps the worst of the love blocks—certainly one of the most pervasive—is the inability to love oneself. This one usually starts with excessive criticism by early childhood authorities, particularly parents. It's amply reinforced by the false modesty society fosters within us, the idea that one must underplay one's accomplishments and self-worth. A pernicious aspect of this cultural hang-up is that self-love is considered the same as selfishness and egotism. Actually, the healthy attitude is to be openly proud of one's achievements. Self-love and selfishness are actually opposites. The egotistical personality feels he doesn't deserve the best, so he grasps and grabs for things selfishly. In contrast, the self-lover is open and generous, knowing good things will always flow his way, sooner or later.

Being unable to love oneself goes hand in hand with poor self-image and low self-esteem. Someone suffering from such love blocks feels he doesn't really deserve love, and this attitude, however unconscious, will keep love away from him. Even if love should somehow come his way, he may feel inside that "the bubble has to burst," and it usually does. We tend to draw circumstances to us which reflect our inner self-image, and if this is poor, our outer conditions will also be. So it really makes practical sense to try to root out negative feelings about yourself.

THE PLEASURE BOOK

   While people tend to believe that they can love others without loving themselves, this is really not true. You can only give what you have inside, and if you're bankrupt in self-love, it's hard to see how you can extend love to others. Attachments or needs, perhaps, but not love. Self-love starts with self-acceptance, simply accepting yourself with all your faults, shortcomings and blemishes. From there you move on to an appreciation of your good points, and a recognition of your unlimited potential for growth. Eventually, you arrive at a place where you can respect, honor and esteem your unique self, without being egotistical or vain.

   Another common love block is the commitment phobia. This often begins in childhood with an overbearing parent. This figure may have exercised rigid control, and there may be a lingering fear of being similarly controlled in love. This leads to a fear of closeness, intimacy or commitment. It doesn't always surface right away. You may be quite romantic in the early stages of an affair, but once you begin growing really close, you start to feel like a cage is closing around you. At that point, many people exit from what might have been an overwhelmingly rewarding involvement.

   Coping with commitment phobia involves relaxing into the relationship and not getting caught up in fear about the future. Remember, no commitment is ironclad. Long-term relationships and marriages dissolve on a daily basis. There's no involvement you can't get free of if you really need to. Commitments should cer-

tainly not be undertaken lightly, but neither should they be shunned because of irrational fears. If you feel overwhelmed or overawed by your lover, examine yourself to see if these are not just childhood plots being replayed. If they are, just relax, stay open and receptive, and roll with the emotional tide. Try getting closer and you may find the fears actually fade.

Another key love block is the fear of rejection. This one usually stems from some past hurt in love. It can paralyze you from taking any risks to reach out to someone new, or to get closer to a current flame. There are many ways to deal with rejection fears. One of the best is to look at what you're losing by *not* taking a chance. Each time someone special comes into your life, you have a golden opportunity for a heaven-sent involvement. But each time you refuse to reach out, that opportunity is lost. The person may have been dying to know you better, but your fears kept you from making the link. The fact is, rejection should not be taken so personally. We all have different needs and desires, and even the most conventionally attractive person will not appeal to everyone. Finding a good lover is sometimes not much more difficult than continuing to knock on doors till one opens. There are plenty of ideal matchups out there for each of us; it's mostly a question of not getting discouraged.

Once you master your love hang-ups, you then have to decide the form of love that most entices you. Your lover should be your ideal pleasure partner, the one who shares your ecstasy explorations to the fullest. It takes quite some time and energy to build the level of trust, confidence and openness to establish this, which is why a conventional commitment makes a lot of sense. A commitment is a long-term engagement which promotes the closeness and acceptance needed with a pleasure partner. Ultimate pleasure pursuits are really only possible in situations

THE PLEASURE BOOK

which are more than merely casual. However, the type of commitment can vary. Commitments are by no means limited to traditional marriage or monogamy. You can commit yourself to someone without fully merging your lives.

Commitments need not be total, nor need they even be defined as a conventional "lovership." You can commit yourself to a continuing friendship with a member of the opposite sex, a relationship which can involve intense sexuality, as I outlined in my June 1982 *Gallery* article, "Sexy Friendships." You can also commit yourself in different ways to different people. For instance, if you and your friend are both involved in time-consuming careers, you may become "part-time lovers" who get together when convenient. While it's not the easiest arrangement to handle, it is possible to have several part-time lovers or sexy friends, each of whom gives you something different. Such arrangements can be quite sensible when you're not emotionally prepared for a fuller commitment.

But whatever style of love you choose, an intimate part of it should be a "pleasure pact." This means you explicitly agree to explore enjoyable experiences to the fullest extent possible. You become conspirators in ecstasy, soulmates in sensuality. Your pact includes being receptive to each other's fantasies and ideas about epicurean activities. You both become bliss-seekers who hunt the world for new joys to share. You jointly establish rituals, forge sensual fantasies and act out erotic roles together. As you creatively follow this course over time, the ties between you will thicken. You'll become united in your own unique "pleasure bond."

What do you do if you don't currently have a love commitment? Or if your present lover is far from being an ideal pleasure partner? The techniques are the same in both cases. *You create a love relationship by being a loving person.* There is indeed a tender art of loving which can be learned and practiced. Once you master it, you may find yourself irresistible! It has little to do with looks, power, prestige, status or money. Put very simply, it can be summed up in four words: being a nice person.

In practice, this means being thoughtful, empathetic, sincere and willing to please. It means getting beyond your own hang-ups and ego blocks to *understand what the other person wants,* not what you think he wants. It consists of catering

to the person's unique desires and needs as he or she conceives them. Naturally, being a pleasure philosopher goes a long way here. The bliss-seeker is already attuned to the fantasies, hungers and appetites of others, because these teach him new ways to enhance his own experiences. When wooing a potential lover, he has open ears for the person's cravings, kinks, lusts and aspirations. He'll want to know all about the things which turn his new friend on. So one of the key rules of the art of loving is creative listening.

Once you learn the things that spark your friend, you can then program your attentions for his individual predilections. The gifts you give will reflect this personalized approach. For example, an astrology buff will appreciate a thin paperback on his birth sign a lot more than that bestseller *everyone's* reading. You can also make sure to involve yourself in areas of interest to your friend, and to integrate yourself into his or her social circle.

Little reminders of your love also go a long way. Phone calls just to say hello, sweetheart notes left under the pillow, "sensitivity cards" sent for no occasion at all—efforts like these show how much you care. Being responsible and considerate also count. Show up on time, dress appropriately, be courteous to his or her family and friends. Don't be a drain on his energies, but a positive uplift. If your dating has caused time problems for a lover, for example, offer a helping hand. Suggest a "work party" in which you straighten out some chores together while talking and sharing some drinks. Always treat the person as you would be treated—with kindness, caring and consideration—and you'll be amazed how often your favors will be returned, with added dividends. Only the coldest, most hardhearted individual will not respond to this "Golden Rule" approach—and you surely can live without someone like that.

Over time, your friend will respond to your efforts with overtures of closeness and commitment. When that occurs, be receptive and responsive. Always reward attempts to get close with renewed attentions on your part. In essence, being a nice person boils down to "doing the little things," making numerous loving gestures which add up. In the wonderful world of love, intimacy and human warmth, nice people just about always finish first.

This simple rule of being nice will work wonders in virtually all love contexts, whether it's in a relationship, or with family, friends, etc. The hustlers, shysters and rip-off artists may do well in the smoke-filled boardrooms or on the streets, but they won't find their games nearly so handy for winning love. The "looking out for number one" credo, so prevalent today, may work for a few short-run points, but in the long term it only leads to isolation, emptiness and alienation. The true pleasure philosopher is not a naive narcissist who believes the way to be loved is have others fawning all over him. The intelligent bliss-seeker knows the difference between being loved for what one *does* or the position one occupies in society and being loved for what one *is* inside, apart from credentials, fame, fortune, etc.

The pleasure philosopher looks for love in all his involvements, not just in sexual relationships. He'll do his best to give and receive tender caring with family and friends, and may even find love permeating his work efforts. There are many ways to locate love at work apart from the literal pursuit of affairs with coworkers (a dubious effort at best; office affairs have a high mortality rate and can lead to nasty repercussions). One can be enraptured with the work itself, as many people in the creative trades can testify to. People in the helping professions often become deeply committed to the clients in their care. Teachers may empathize with and aid their students' educational growth. Social workers may show complete compassion for their clients' welfare.

Children and pets can be tremendous outlets for the love impulses. Both groups are exempt from various taboos society places on affection, so they can be rich sources of warmth and tenderness. Most parents take great pride and pleasure in seeing their kids unfold, while pets are almost a universal fountain of nurturance. Stroking the soft fur of pets has been shown to lower the pulse beat and heart rate, reducing stress and the risk of coronary fatalities. Beyond being soft and cuddly, pets also give unconditional love, so rare among people. The dog or cat doesn't care whether you're old, ugly, deformed, unshaven or disheveled—they purr and snuggle against you no matter what shape you're in. Society has just begun to discover the wonderfully therapeutic value of pets, as they're now being used to bring tangible love into the lives of isolated, lonely people like prison inmates, mental patients and the institutionalized elderly.

Perhaps the highest form of love—one few people understand or appreciate—is universal or brotherly love. This is the experience of feeling kinship with all of creation—with humanity, nature, plants, animals, the cosmos—and feeling that you're intimately connected with all of existence. You find this feeling very prevalent among American Indian groups. This is the type of love rhapsodized by saints, sages, prophets and mystics, but it's something the pleasure philosopher can appreciate as well in everyday life. This love usually leads to a commitment to higher principles and causes. For instance, the universal lover may become involved in fighting world hunger, social injustice, poverty, ecological abuse and war. He may do volunteer work in the community, support minority causes, civil liberties or other social concerns. This selfless devotion to ideas and efforts larger than one's own narrow interests produces an intense inner glow, a warm internal sensation that one is flowing in harmony with the universe, living in tune with the Tao, as they say in China. Jesus, when asked to summarize the essential teachings of the Ten Commandments, said that we should love God with all our heart and love our neighbor as ourselves. This is one of the best formulations of universal/brotherly love, a sentiment every bliss-seeker should appreciate, endorse and practice.

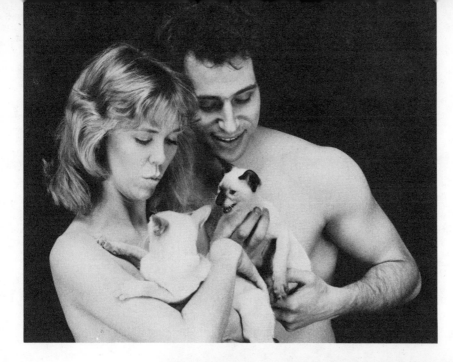

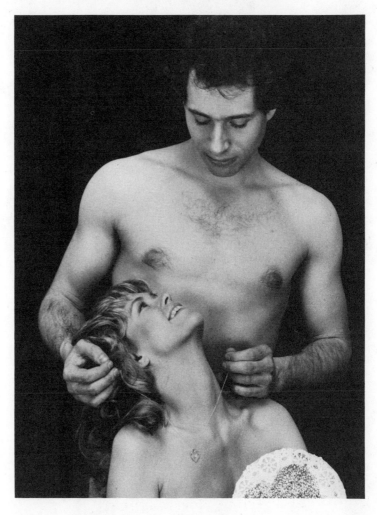

10

The Healthy Hedonist

Poor health is one of the major blocks to the average bliss-seeker in our society. Most people who pursue sense gratification are totally undisciplined in their approach. They eat what they want, drink excessively, doing anything and everything to their bodies regardless of the consequences. Over time, these excesses wear away at them, producing pain, discomfort and bad habits. The senses become dulled, and ever-increasing stimulation is needed to feel anything. You may become sick, run down or habituated to harmful substances. These are hardly ideal conditions to appreciate pleasure.

The healthy hedonist is a viable alternative to his undisciplined counterpart. The healthy hedonist realizes that a strong, sound body and mind are needed for full sense enjoyment. Healthy people actually have the deepest capacity for pleasure. Fitness forges the human instrument into a finely honed pleasure mechanism, boosting the body's ability to sustain peak pleasure states. The run-down individual is simply incapable of enduring long, intense pleasure bouts which the healthy hedonist handles easily.

Pursuing a healthy lifestyle does not have to involve drudgery. Actually, exercise can be a form of play, and it's only deep-seated antifitness attitudes which make it seem like hard work. As already indicated, strenuous exercise releases natural opiates in the brain, the endorphins. When you run, swim, bike, play vigorous team sports or the like, your brain is stimulated by these endorphins, which calm, relax and reduce pain. This fact alone is a great reason to launch an exercise program. When you work out, it's like pushing a pleasure button in the brain! And that's just one of the benefits of being fit.

Exercise, especially aerobic (deep-breathing) activities, also increases circulation, enhances respiration, loosens fatty deposits and rids your system of poisons. All these effects will greatly increase your ecstasy abilities. The healthy hedonist has a more vivid sense of aliveness. He can savor his pleasures over longer spans, lengthen his lovemaking sessions, stretch out his enjoyment interludes. His fitness also permits him to survive all kinds of pleasure orgies with no sweat.

For example, let's say he's set out on an erotic ecstasy episode which will involve drinking and lovemaking till the wee hours. His well-conditioned body will be able to bounce right back. Fitness also contributes to a clear mind by helping eliminate accumulated toxins. A clear head helps make you practical, sensible and better able to appreciate life's beauties and wonders. Another key benefit of working out is improved physical appearance. You become trimmer, tighter and straighter in build. Muscle tone improves while fatty deposits disappear. Your skin will become smoother and rosier. You'll be much nicer to look at and touch. Pleasure-seekers are always interested in drawing exciting, interesting people to them, and being more attractive is one of the best ways to do that.

But exercise is only one way to improve health. You can also cut down on the harmful things you're doing to your body. This includes being sensible about the junk you put into it. Poor diet is one of the chief causes of feeling run-down. Trying to live off junk food is like feeding watered-down gas to a high-performance engine. Most American diets contain far too much salt, refined sugar and fat.

There are many healthy diets one can try, and these can be learned about in publications like *Whole Life Times* and *Health and Diet Times* (available at health food stores, as are many excellent books on diet and nutrition). But if you don't want to get involved in elaborate diet planning, there are some simple rules to follow. Balance is the key to healthy eating. Choose your diet among the different food groups like fruits, vegetables, grains and proteins. By regularly getting

74

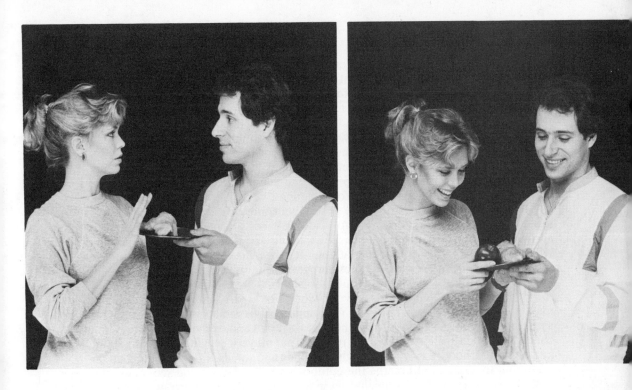

"square meals" with all the major food groups included, you assure yourself of adequate nutrition. Another rule is to cut down on harmful foods. These include refined sugar products (cake, candy, table sugar), fatty meats and highly processed foods (white bread, most prepackaged products).

You don't have to be a purist and totally eliminate such foods, just cut back on them. They cause all sorts of problems like interfering with digestion, raising havoc with blood-sugar levels, and generally bogging down your system. It's better to stick with natural foods like whole-grain breads and cereals, sprouts and fresh fruits and vegetables. But what if you're irresistibly addicted to candy bars? There is a compromise position: eat the junk food, but balance it with a natural food. For example, follow your junk binge with a cleansing, healthy food like an apple, celery, carrot or sprouts. These will help temper the harsh effects of the offending food, and may restore lost nutrients at the same time.

You can use a similar balancing act with other harmful activities and excesses. Let's say you're absolutely wedded to heavy partying: long hours filled with lots of drinking, smoking, loud music, etc. Ideally, it would be best to moderate things, especially with thoroughly deleterious activities like tobacco smoking. Smoking dulls your senses, slicing your pleasure abilities drastically; it also cuts breath, making it tough to complete an exercise program. But if you must continue your frenzied pace, you can blunt its effects through regular workouts. After resting up, get out and exercise, and this will reverse many of the shocks on your system. You can cut corners in lots of ways when you're physically fit.

There are many excellent exercise modes to choose from, and one should ideally suit your temperament. People who are serene and quiet may prefer yoga, while bouncy, active types may like calisthenics, swimming or short-distance running. Long-distance jogging and marathon running appeal to those who enjoy nature and contemplation. Powerful, macho sorts may delight in weight training and the martial arts like karate and kung fu. Graceful, expressive types will enjoy aerobic dance and tai chi. Practical, down-to-earth individuals may appreciate

75

cycling, which allows you to work out while getting to some destination. Some people benefit by combining different exercise styles for maximum fitness.

My own privately developed workout routine includes calisthenics and stretching to warm up, followed by heavy upper-body work for muscle strength (push-ups, tension coils or weights, depending upon available equipment), then sit-ups and leg-raises to trim the lower body. I finish up with yoga postures for flexibility and limbering. I do this routine each morning upon arising, and although it lasts less than a half-hour (no rest between movements at all), it never fails to get my day springing, even on a short sleep span. For stamina, I commute on a bicycle and do fast-paced three-mile runs. You'll notice I've said little about competitive sports thus far. That's because these generally cannot be counted on for physical fitness. Most team sports do not involve disciplined, sustained exercise, but on-and-off movements. For example, baseball, tennis and football all involve periods when you stand around and do nothing. It's best to think of team sports as recreation and leave the serious fitness program to individualized exercise.

Whatever activity you choose, you'll soon learn that the right attitude is crucial to your success. If you approach your workouts as drudgery—something you must do—you'll give up in no time. Your approach should be positive. Imagine it as giving yourself the gift of life and health. Be joyful and exuberant, like a young child at play. For instance, if you're running, put on your jogging suit and get out in the neighborhood, enjoy all the sights, sounds and smells. Don't get hung up on aches and tiredness, but breathe the outdoor air, marvel at all you see, enjoy the ever-shifting scenes. This is meditation in motion. When you finish up, feel good about your accomplishment.

Another attitudinal trick is to link your workout with your future pleasure pursuits. You can use pleasure as a reward for your fitness efforts. I know one fellow who works out especially hard on days when he's about to throw one of his elaborate parties. "When I'm running, I think of the partying I'm going to be doing tonight," he says. "The better my effort, the more I allow myself to bust loose later." You can also make an *indirect* connection between exercise and enjoyment. You can see yourself as gradually building your body into an exquisitely sensitive, well-tuned pleasure instrument. Each workout makes you a more potent repository for bliss. See yourself in that light and the workouts will become much more rewarding.

The difference between the healthy and unhealthy hedonist has to be felt to be really appreciated. One of the great joys in life is to have a fluid, graceful, flexible, sound body. You can then move easily and agilely, giving you added freedom for all your bliss seeking. Both body and mind will reflect a brighter, livelier, more attractive you, which will boost your self-image and draw people to you. You'll view life through clearer eyes and an unclouded mind. You'll exude greater self-discipline, inner control and self-mastery. Your success in building and maintaining a steady exercise program will soon translate into successes in all walks of life.

If you happen to be an extremely *unhealthy* hedonist presently, you may be facing the common dilemma about public exposure during exercise. This is especially a problem for very obese people. The skinny or muscular body type may look fine jogging around the park, on a cycle, or in the gym, while the overweight frame may seem way out of place. I've known some heavy people just starting a fitness program who've been subject to snappy insults by nasty passersby or even other fitness-seekers. So the out-of-shape individual faces a real problem, because the very activities he most needs to firm up could lead to public ostracism, which can easily destroy his enthusiasm and positive efforts. The best solution to this problem is to put together an effective at-home routine before venturing into the public. And luckily, there are many sound ways to do this.

Some fitness techniques are easily adapted to individual home use, with little more than an exercise mat or thick rug. Calisthenics, yoga and aerobic dancing are just a few examples. You can pick up a detailed guidebook on one of these subjects and follow the instructions step by step in full privacy. There are also tapes and records for instruction in these areas, as well as music to accompany your workouts. If you want to make a further commitment, you can explore the large variety of home exercise equipment. A lavish spender could set up an all-purpose Universal or Nautilus weight-training gym in his own basement. More modest expenditures will include a barbell set and a padded exercise bench to work the chest, arms, shoulders and legs. Add a slant board, and you can cover the abdominal and midsection muscles.

There are other types of equipment which will build strength and/or stamina. Skip-joggers give you aerobic benefits as you run in place on a trampolinelike surface. Rowing machines provide aerobic fitness while building upper-body strength as well. There are stationary bicycles, isometric gadgets for strength (like the "Bullworker," good for chest and arm development) and compact hydraulic-pump equipment which mimics the effects of weight training. Diversified Products of Compton, California, has a particularly attractive piece of hydraulic-pressure hardware, the "Bodywork 300," which converts from an aerobic rower to weight-training device for under two hundred dollars.

An even cheaper investment I've personally gotten lots of mileage from is AMF's "Whitely 6-Way Home Gym." This gadget uses tension springs to duplicate the effects of much more expensive weight-training and isometric equipment. The compact unit can be set up to do the work of barbells, dumbells, wall pulleys, etc., and even comes with hand grips for forearm development. In a year's time of regular use along with other exercises like yoga, these simple little springs have expanded my chest size about eight inches and my arms about three inches, and we're not talking about fat either. Not bad for a cost of around thirty dollars.

Many of these products can be perused at sporting-goods stores or large health food chains like GNC. You can also see ads for them in health publications like *Whole Life Times,* bodybuilding magazines, and high-tech product catalogs like the *Sharper Image* of San Francisco. They are generally space saving, inexpensive and produce many of the same results as workouts at a gym or health club. I think they can take you just so far in terms of ultimate development and fitness, but they can help trim and shape you to the point where you can move on to public exercise pursuits without fear of embarrassment. Once you reach that point, you're well on your way to a lifestyle of healthy hedonism.

Recreation and Relaxation

The pleasure philosopher appreciates the value of good, clean fun. He sees life as a delicate balance between work and rest, intense activity and light, pleasant pursuits. He knows that he needs regular breaks from life's daily routines. This is where recreation fits in. The pleasure philosopher makes sure he schedules enough "rec time" during his busy week.

Recreation can be part of an overall fitness program, but unlike an exercise routine, it does not have a disciplined, dedicated focus. Its aim is different. You're not trying to build a sound body, though that may be a benefit, but simply enjoy yourself. You're escaping the rigorous pressures of everyday existence. It will keep you from burning out from overwork, stress and all the other ills of modern life. Recreation can take many forms. Some people enjoy their exercise routine enough for it alone to serve as recreation, though most require a lighter alternative.

For many, competitive sports serve as a useful outlet. Tennis, bowling, golf, volleyball, basketball, football, baseball and softball are all excellent examples. Competitive sports are mini-worlds with their own rules, and you can learn a lot about group cooperation from them. They provide an opportunity to express yourself in different symbolic roles, like leader, hero and savior. They also let you taste bitter roles like loser and scapegoat in the safe confines of a play world. However, it's crucial not to get hung up on the winning-and-losing aspect of sports. These are times to experiment and be adventurous, not to get caught up in conventional competition. Remember, the idea is to escape the real world, not replicate it.

Certain sports allow you to deepen your relationship with primary pleasure partners. Some couples derive a great deal of closeness from exercising together, for instance, jogging or doing yoga. Certain competitive sports, like tennis, bowling and golf, allow you to either team up with your pleasure partner or compete with him directly. You can learn a lot about your feelings for each other in such matchups. You may become more closely bonded, or uncover areas where your feelings are unresolved. Another popular shared recreation is dance. Over the ages, dance has been a potent courting ritual—a key ceremonial rite, a powerful means of self-expression. Couples can heighten and deepen their feelings for each other through dance.

Recreation can also be enjoyed outside the province of sports and competition. Getting out of doors into nature is an age-old restorative remedy. Being in natural settings clears the mind, restores oxygen to the blood and refreshes the spirit. Some people enjoy vigorous outdoor pursuits like hiking, skiing and climbing, while others prefer restful, "do-nothing" hanging out. You can choose from picnics, boating, fishing and camping. Whatever you pick, it's important to be in a

setting that calms and relaxes you. Beautiful beaches, majestic mountains, babbling brooks, fertile forests, serene seashores—all of these will help heal and rejuvenate you. It pays to share such scenic wonders with special friends and intimate pleasure partners.

It's also possible to pursue recreation apart from either sports or nature. Many popular pastime activities can serve some of the same functions as recreation. Games like chess, checkers, backgammon and the like can take you away from everyday concerns. So can listening to music, reading and working with personal computers. Video games, radio, newspapers and TV are diversions for many, but you have to be cautious with most mass-market entertainment. The pleasure philosopher is always sensitive to prepackaged pseudopleasures which lull, hypnotize and take large amounts of valuable time from real pleasures.

Most mass-market entertainment puts out values that bliss-seekers prefer not to traffic in. Violence, hatred, conflict, hopelessness and degradation are all messages that are constantly focused on in the media. You will certainly find scant genuine human pleasure in TV sitcoms, "shoot 'em up" video games or the news. It pays to be more selective when seeking popular entertainment. Quality films, theater, concerts, opera and dance are all better alternatives. If TV is a "must" with you, you might try obtaining a video recorder so you can selectively tape your own programming or play prerecorded videocassettes of your own choice. Any intelligent self-selection is preferable to mindlessly accepting what the media feeds to you.

An intelligent recreation program makes ample use of relaxation time. It's important to get regular relaxation apart from exercise or recreation. Stress has become the key killer of our times, and is closely connected with many life-threatening illnesses. Stress has a cumulative effect, and will cause the system to break down if left unrelieved over long stretches. Relaxation is one of the most potent antidotes for stress. A regular relaxation routine works wonders in restoring spent energies and rebuilding tired tissues. It prevents burnout and overload.

Restful sleep is one of the great relaxants. It pays to keep as close to a planned sleep schedule as possible. First you gauge how much sleep your body needs—many get by with less than the standard eight hours; some require more. Do this by varying your sleep span for a while. You know you've slept enough when you can carry out daily activities without a sense of fatigue. Once you have determined your ideal sleep time, try to get this amount by staying close to a sleep schedule. Go to sleep and wake up about the same general time each day. Try not to oversleep when you've been up late the night before, as this can throw off your internal clock and knock your hard-won sleep schedule way off course.

The same goes for lengthy naps. If you've gotten insufficient sleep the night before, a long nap can really throw off your normal sleep time. You'll be awake and alert when it's time to doze that night, which will only aggravate the problem. It's better to gut it out and avoid napping, getting to bed earlier the next night to "catch up." Another good alternative is to learn a meditation technique and practice it twice a day, morning and early evening. The evening meditation will always refresh and relax you, accomplishing the same thing in twenty minutes that an hour-plus nap will do. There are many excellent books, tapes and programs for learning the art of meditation. Studies link it with reducing tension, calming the mind and thinking clearer.

Meditation can also be profitably employed when you experience insomnia. You can sit up in bed and practice your technique, easing your mind so that you can sink into a comfortable slumber. Another way to cope with insomnia is a technique called "progressive relaxation." This involves consciously relaxing each body part, from toe to head, while sitting or lying down. As you work your

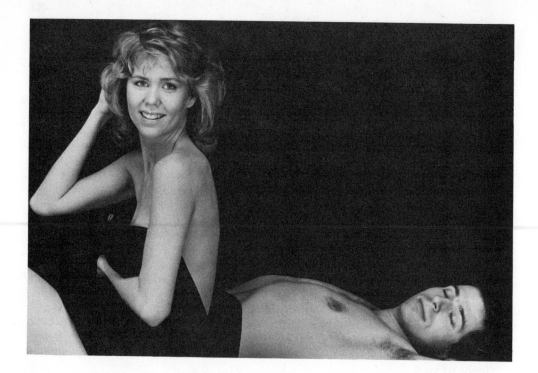

way up your body, you experience a spreading wave of calmness. You eventually drift off into a loose, floating state of serenity, permitting peaceful sleep to follow naturally.

There are two main variations on progressive relaxation. One involves tensing each muscle, then relaxing it. This allows you to experience the contrast between stress and rest, and helps you let go of tension trapped in different body parts. The second variation has you mentally search for tension in each muscle, then consciously tell the muscle to relax. Both methods have you focus your mind on relaxing each area of the body, usually starting with the toes. It may sound overly simplistic, but it's amazing how well it works. By the time you reach your head, your entire body feels loose, limp and flaccid, sort of like floating on a cozy, supportive cloud. Once you reach that state of perfect calmness, you can either drift off to sleep, or get up and do whatever you want. Progressive relaxation is not only an aid to insomnia, but can be used to restore and rejuvenate you at any time. During the day, a regular relaxation routine will serve many of the same functions as meditation.

There are many fine books available on relaxation (some listed under "self-hypnosis") and you can usually locate a good selection through health food stores, Eastern bookshops, or publications like *Whole Life Times.* Many people like to tape a relaxation program onto a cassette, then play it back when they need it. Late at night you can avoid disturbing others by using a "pillow speaker," a small earphone device made for inserting under a pillow. There are also prerecorded tapes available, some of which use soft music to assist the relaxation response. Tapes can usually be obtained at the same places mentioned above.

Whatever meditation or relaxation program appeals to you, it pays to practice it on a daily basis. Over time, you'll find that it builds a calmer, more centered, more serene outlook. When storms whirl around you, you'll tend to keep your head better than before. Your thinking grows clearer, decision making becomes easier and you're more protected against stress-related disorders. You'll find that others admire someone who remains unperturbed and unfrenzied during trying times. An unhurried, steady state of mind will also allow you to savor your pleasure experiences even more. A bliss-seeker with a relaxed, mellow mind is a tough act to beat!

Naturally, you needn't limit yourself to the recreation and relaxation methods presented thus far. The basic rule is to do whatever works for you. Individual preferences and conditioning play key roles here. To find out what R&R activities come naturally to you, simply examine the way you've coped with tension in the past. For example, research reveals that infants exposed to sounds which mimic the heartbeat of the mother will usually become serene and pacified. This is because the heartbeat was a constant feature of the cozy, safe world of the womb which the baby just emerged from. Some observers feel that this early conditioning is responsible for the almost universal human response to music. While musical tastes vary widely, all people enjoy some combination of rhythm and meter.

But that doesn't mean that *you* as an individual will. While music may act as stimulating recreation or soothing relaxation for some, that may simply not be true for you. Going to football games or doing crossword puzzles might well be your particular cup of tea. When examining your preferences, try to separate harmful R&R activities from safe ones. It's very easy to form habits which pacify temporarily but do serious long-range harm. For example, lots of people claim that cigarette smoking "relaxes" them. But is this genuine enjoyment or an addiction masquerading as such?

Cigarette smoking can definitely serve a lot of functions which seem to have calming effects. Playing with one's fingers and putting something in one's mouth are common ways babies give themselves strokes. Smoking also sates oral cravings, not only in the thumb-sucking sense, but also because deeply inhaled smoke gives you a sensation of being "filled up" inside. Actually, the physiological effects of smoking are exactly the opposite of stress reduction. The nicotine and other irritants really produce excitement and tension, and can even contribute to insom-

nia. But that's hardly the worst they can do: broken skin capillaries, facial wrinkles, breath disorders and cancer are a few of the hazards waiting for you. Cigarettes are probably the prime example of a pseudopleasure.

But even more uplifting activities can be nonrelaxing if your attitude toward them is bad. For instance, vacations ought to be ideal ways to unwind and attain much-needed rest, relaxation and recreation. But unfortunately, many of us become obsessive about them, especially if we're bogged down with jobs that bore us to tears. We may spend most of the year planning and shopping around for the perfect vacation package, then once we've found it, spend even more time daydreaming about how wonderful it's going to be. We stop living in the now to dwell in a fantasy future. Our expectations grow so high that there's bound to be a letdown.

Our upcoming "ideal" vacation may ultimately become a real burden, as we meticulously plan each detail, trying to anticipate all our wants and needs in a situation we picked, ironically enough, for its novelty and newness. We may worry about having the right clothes, fitting in with the crowd, knowing the local lingo, getting sick, etc. Then finally the magic day arrives and we're there in our special retreat. Problem is, no fantasy island or love boat can live up to our months-long preconceptions. It's common for Americans to begin begrudging their trips after a short while. They start to think about their jobs and the folks back home, and pretty soon they're finding fault with the vacation. They may feel they're "roughing it" too much, or that service is bad, the food's no good, the boat's rocking too much, etc. Then the rest of the time is usually spent trying to capture "for memory's sake" the very vacation they're frowning upon. Cameras, movie equipment, tapes, etc., are used to immortalize themselves in settings they can hardly stand anymore. Precious time gets gobbled up trying to preserve the facade of "having a great time" for the hometown friends and family. Meanwhile, the reality of the vacation and its many growth opportunities get lost in the shuffle.

Of course, this perfectionist attitude can pervade any R&R pursuit. Trying to create the "perfect" anything is a real losing affair, whether it be a trip, date, game, meditation practice, etc. Exceedingly high expectations inevitably lead to disappointment. They contribute to stress, the exact opposite result you expect from R&R activities. It's much healthier to have a "hang loose, let's see what comes up" attitude towards R&R and life in general. Peace of mind comes from an unbiased, flexible, noncontrolling viewpoint. "Go with the flow," as the gurus say.

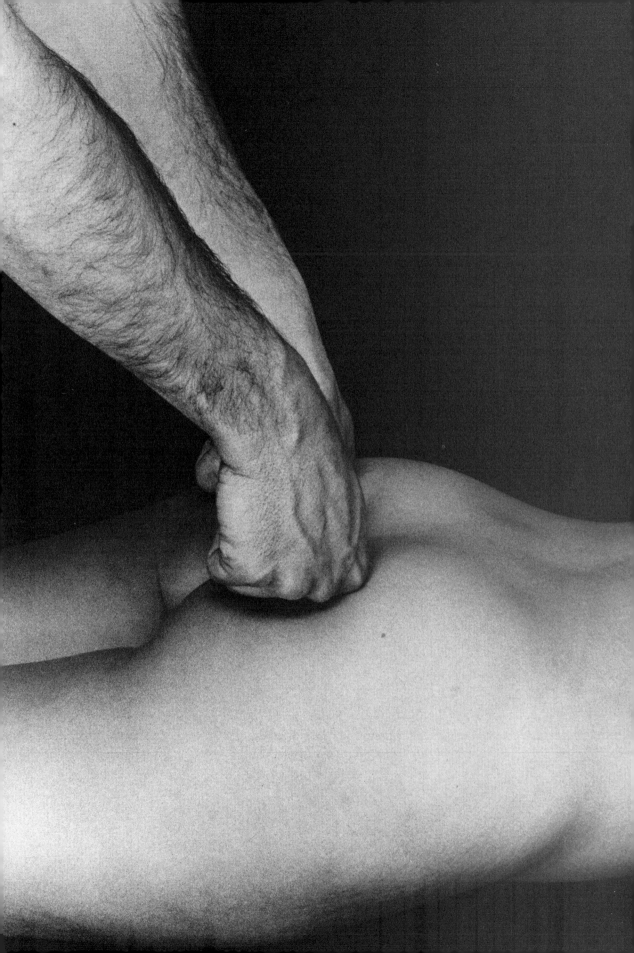

12

Bodywork

Restoration of spent energies is crucial for the bliss-seeker. He burns more energy than the average individual in his varied pleasure pursuits. Exercise, recreation and relaxation are all ways to rest and recuperate, but there's a quicker route to recharge your batteries. Bodywork is a collection of techniques designed to release trapped energy, thus invigorating and enlivening you. There are all types of bodywork, but the techniques described in this chapter are simple and well suited for practice with a close pleasure partner. You can incorporate them into your sensuality and "sexplorations," perhaps as part of a massage routine. The techniques themselves can result in highly pleasurable sensations of relaxation, rest, peace and serenity.

The origins of bodywork trace back to ancient Oriental medicine, and are related to acupuncture. Chinese medicine viewed disease and discomfort as signs of trapped energy in the body. They put together a model of the body divided by a number of energy circuits ("meridians") which coursed throughout the body, connecting various glands and organs with points on the skin. Basic life energies circulated through these meridians, but blockages in the flow resulted in illness. These blockages were treated by putting pressure on the points on the skin which were linked with the meridian in question. Acupuncture needles were inserted into the skin to stimulate these points. Recent research has revealed that acupuncture provides a great deal of symptom relief, including those problems that standard medicine has no remedies for.

You don't need needles, however, to do bodywork. The same points can also be stimulated by finger pressure. Shiatsu, which was introduced to Japan in the sixth century by Buddhist monks from China, is a popular system employing thumb pressure for the same effects as acupuncture. Reflexology is a Westernized version of shiatsu which mainly focuses on pressure points in the hands and feet. Before describing these techniques, it's worth mentioning more recent research on bodywork which helps explain how it works. Psychologist Wilhelm Reich performed pioneering experiments on the nature of the life force throughout the 1950s. He invented the term "body armor" to show how repressed desires and needs become trapped inside different areas of the body. As children, we were not allowed to express certain needs, especially sexual ones. The movements associated with the repression of these forbidden drives became frozen in the tissues over many years. This resulted in tight, shortened muscles which impeded proper posture and movement.

Reich learned that certain manipulations, like deep-muscle massage, could actually release repressed tension and the memories associated with it. Patients sometimes relived early traumas when a particular body part was worked on. Other bodywork technicians found this effect as well. Deep-tissue manipulations like rolfing sometimes resulted in the release of a flood of pent-up frustrations and associated childhood memories. This turned conventional psychotherapy on its head. The usual method used in therapy had been *talking* (psychoanalysis) to uncover repressed feelings, but bodyworkers were often getting quicker results by *touching*. The emotional catharsis which bodywork can bring is valuable to the dedicated bliss-seeker. The less repressed baggage you carry inside, the freer your pleasure explorations can be.

Shiatsu should ideally be done on a padded massage table, but you can use a bed. The work is done with the balls of the thumbs. Use both thumbs at once, applying pressure by extending your arms straight out and leaning in with your *body weight. Don't* use muscle pressure, as this will tire you out in no time. You should continue applying pressure to each point for three to five seconds, and the shiatsu manuals recommend twelve to fifteen pounds of pressure per thumb (you can test this on a bathroom scale). That's a lot of pressure, so you may want to use less until you get the hang of it. However, deep pressure is the key to shiatsu's benefits. You want to invoke a "pleasure/pain" response your partner can *really feel,* not just superficial surface stimulation.

Shiatsu is really a rejuvenation technique whose benefits come from releasing trapped tension. After a treatment, you'll feel looser, livelier and more relaxed. However, the healing quality of shiatsu doesn't preclude making it a sensual event. You can create a cozy, romantic setting, including full nudity for both partners, soft music and lighting, incense and pleasant drinks. You can combine shiatsu with sensual massage or make it a part of your lovemaking rituals. You can take turns giving and receiving, or alternate the roles from session to session. Use your fertile imagination to transform shiatsu into a sacred ceremony of love and delight!

Space considerations prevent us from outlining a full shiatsu routine. For that, refer to the step-by-step approach in my book, *The Joy of Touch* (Simon & Schuster, 1981). What we'll do here is set out the initial movements in a shiatsu program, then tell you how to apply the general techniques to other areas. The first shiatsu move is finger pressure along the spine. Begin at the top of the back, placing your thumbs alongside the spine, about an inch to each side. Press down the length of the spine an inch at a time. Keep your arms straight, leaning in with your body weight when pressing. Don't press directly on the spinal column, but to the sides of it. Breathe out when pressing, and in when letting go. As with all shiatsu movements, repeat this two or three times, holding the pressure three to five seconds on each point.

The next area to work on is where the hip bone connects with the spine. Press out along the hipbone an inch at a time to the outer edge of the hip. Next, press down the shoulder blades. Then press from the shoulder blades to the spine in a V-shaped pattern. Next, use the thumb and forefinger of one hand to press down the back of the neck until you reach the spine. Lighten your pressure on the neck.

Press all along the back of the neck and head. Do the head with one hand, using the other for balance. Then switch to the back of the legs, covering all the way from thigh to heel, going light on the back of the knees. You can also try using palm pressure on the legs and buttocks. Now have your partner turn over and lie on his back. Use pressure all over the soles, tops, and sides of the feet. Then press up the calf to the knees, lightening up again on the knee itself. Cover the entire upper thighs, pressing in parallel lines on up. You can work the bony parts of the pelvis with your thumbs, but it's best to use your palms or flats of the fingers on the abdomen. Lighten up there and on the ribcage. Then do the chest and shoulders. For the shoulder muscles, switch back to thumb pressure.

Next, cover each arm completely with thumb and finger pressure, working in

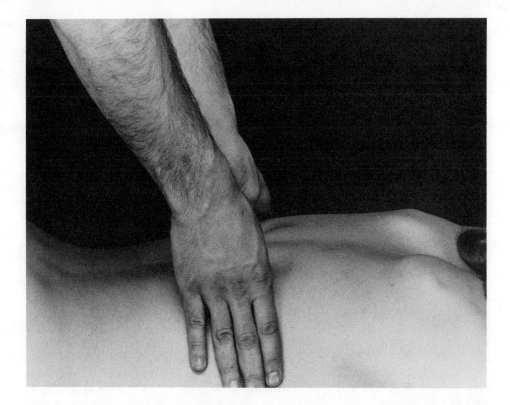

parallel lines from shoulder to wrist. You can support each arm on top of your leg. Now continue along the wrist, then the entire hand. You can cradle your friend's hand between yours, with your thumbs first pressing on his palms, then on the backs of his hands.

For the face, it's best to have your partner sit up so you can control the pressure better. Use light pressure along the sides of the neck, with thumb and forefinger and one hand alongside the windpipe, but not directly on it. Then work the chin and jaw areas, the cheekbones, the eye-socket bone that surrounds the eyes, using delicate pressure. Push in with thumbs on each side of the temple, then finish up on the forehead and the scalp. Shiatsu on the face and head is especially good for sinus problems, eye strain, headaches and hangovers. After completing the routine, you may both want to rest awhile. The giver is usually a bit tired, while the receiver may be drained from the constant release of tension and trapped pressure. Shiatsu takes some getting used to, since the unique pleasure/pain response is something we're not normally exposed to. But it gives a sort of deep-seated gratification, as though your body has been embraced in a strong, yet loving, bear hug. With regular use, you'll undoubtedly feel more energetic and alert, and you may suffer fewer chronic, nagging ailments.

Reflexology is based upon the same principles as shiatsu, but it focuses on the hands and feet. These areas contain some of the key pressure points connected with all the major organs and glands throughout the body. The hands and feet are thought of as miniature representatives of the body, with the top, bottom and midpoints reflecting the corresponding body spots. Left-side body parts are represented on the left hand, with the opposite true for the right hand. Covering both hands or feet will take care of the entire body, so reflexology can be seen as a short form of shiatsu.

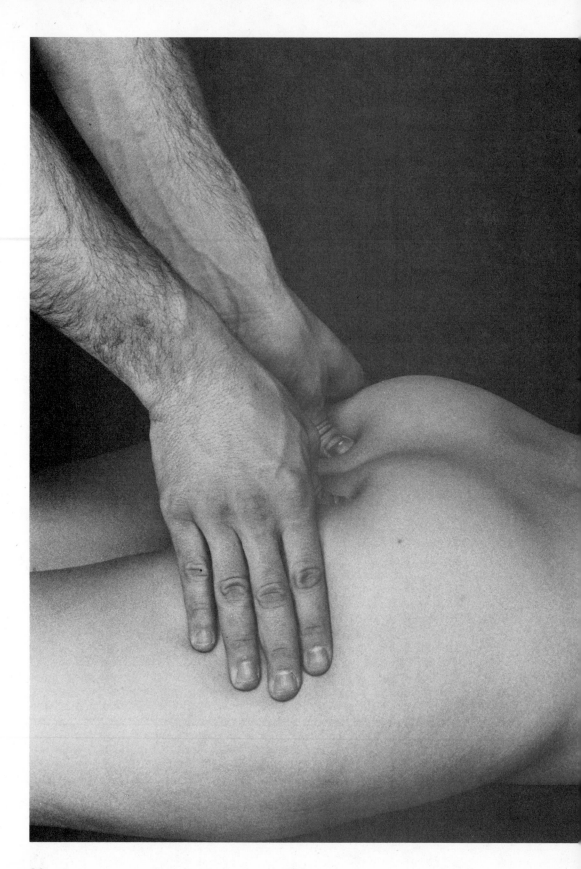

You can use reflexology on yourself or share it with a friend. Since it's not nearly as elaborate as shiatsu, it's easily adapted to situations where you need a quick rejuvenating lift, but just don't have the time or energy for a full shiatsu session. Once again, reflexology can be combined with a romantic setting involving sensual massage, erotic play, etc. You can move from reflexology to massage to sex, going from healing to sensuality to sexuality in one harmonious whole.

People generally report a great deal of enjoyment from hand and foot massage. The basic motion is a pressing, rolling action with thumbs and fingers. Use pressure deep enough to penetrate the skin surface to reach the bones and muscles. The hands and feet reflex to the same body spots, so you get the same benefits from both. It's slightly more effective with the feet, because the larger surface lets you hit more reflex points. Many people use hand massage to work on themselves, saving the more exotic pleasures of foot massage for others. You can share foot or hand massage, or both, with a primary pleasure partner. We'll be briefly sketching a hand-and-foot reflexology schema here. For a full treatment, please refer to my book *The Joy of Touch*.

For the hands, start with the thumbs, then each finger, pressing all over. Then do the soft pad at the base of each finger, the soft spot in front of the thumb, and the outside edge of the hand, by the little finger. Then do the lower part of the palm, the middle parts and all palm areas not yet covered. Next, do the back of the hand and wrist. Do both hands.

For foot massage, use deep, circular, pressing movements. Press as hard as your friend can handle. Start with the big toe, then do the other toes, pressing all over each. Then press on the instep beneath the big toe, all the way down. Next, press the pads under the toes, up and down the center of the sole, making sure you cover all of it. Do the lower part of the sole, all around the heel, then the back of the foot, the ankle, Achilles tendon and the top front of the foot.

A good reflexology routine will release a lot of trapped tension and will leave you feeling soothed and relieved. You'll feel energy coursing through your body as your partner hits key reflex points. This can be the perfect preparation for sensual and sexual expression. With energy flowing freely, you'll be highly receptive to sensual strokes and erotic activities. Bodywork therapies can be neatly woven into any creative pleasure pattern you choose!

Bodywork techniques are not limited to reflexology and shiatsu, though they are two of the simplest do-it-yourself systems. Other popular techniques include somatic massage, rolfing, postural integration, Feldenkrais manipulations, Reiki massage and touch for health. However, most of these require extensive training and can involve intricate, deep-muscle movements which the untrained would be foolhardy to try. But that doesn't mean they must be excluded from your pleasure life. The goal of these methods is to reintegrate your body, remove trapped tensions and literally make you less out of joint. They can assist your overall fitness program, thus increasing your body's ability to appreciate pleasure.

If you're willing to invest in your own well-being, it's not a bad idea to set up regular sessions with a professional bodywork therapist. Since there are quite a variety to choose from, it pays to shop around. The first step is to learn about the system or systems you're interested in trying. Visit a yoga ashram, New Age Center, holistic health center, health food store or metaphysical bookstore and pick up some literature on the subject. There are specific books on each topic, general guidebooks on both techniques and centers where they're practiced and magazines which discuss the methods, like *New Age, Whole Life Times* and the *International Journal of Holistic Health and Medicine*. My own *Joy of Touch* gives detailed instructions about most major bodywork systems, as well as the

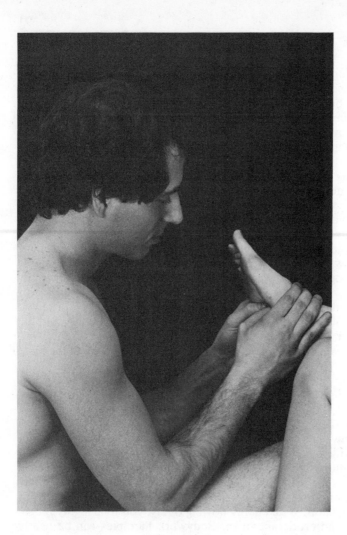

theories behind other systems not described in depth. Many centers, as well as adult education classes, teach the techniques.

Once you've learned what you want, find a good practitioner. The centers where you obtained your information can provide solid leads. Friends who've tried the technique can lend invaluable references. When judging a therapist, check out his or her background carefully. Some bodywork systems have formal training programs, the most elaborate being the three-year education of chiropractors. Some states have licensing requirements, like the M.Th. degree many massage professionals possess. In other cases, the practitioner may have trained at a major bodywork institution, such as the Shiatsu Education Center of America or the Swedish Institute (both in New York). One of the centers I'm affiliated with, New York's East-West Institute for Holistic Studies, offers a master's degree in holistic health. Remember, though, formal training is no guarantee of quality treatment—some of the best healers have had none.

Once you locate a qualified therapist, you have to do what all psychotherapy clients do, check the person out to see if she or he suits you. While the individual may be technically competent, the healing will be hindered if the "vibes" between you are not in synch. Remember, bodywork is an intimate experience in which you'll not only be touched in private areas, but may even be nude. So there should be a good rapport and trust between the two of you, or you may have defensive responses which will interfere with the treatment. Once you've cleared that hurdle, you have to work out a fee schedule and number of sessions. Unlike psychotherapy, which can go on for years, most bodywork practice has a limited number of sessions. This is especially true for deep-tissue manipulations like rolfing or postural integration, where the goal is concrete: realignment of the body.

Bodywork systems with less specific goals, such as general stress reduction, can, however, continue as long as you like. For example, massage therapists usually build up a steady clientele who see them on a regular basis. The massage helps alleviate the accumulated tensions of daily life, and can be quite effective in reducing overall stress. Particularly in modern, frenzied urban settings, regular massage or other bodywork is a highly worthwhile investment in one's health. The cost of the sessions should be weighed against the money spent on standard "junk entertainment" like mindless movies, arcade games, bars, discos, etc.

Actually, if you're really concerned with your budget but still want the benefits of bodywork, there is one free solution: regular exercise, especially yoga. Yoga has been described as the most effective form of self-massage because the varied stretching postures limber and loosen you up, and over time help realign your frame like bodywork does. I know this for a fact, because before I began practicing yoga, I suffered from a protruding disk in my back. Occasionally, the condition would become aggravated and I'd have to use crutches to get around. But from slowly working myself into spinal stretching positions like the plow and cobra, after about a year's time the disk problem virtually disappeared. I gave my crutches away two years ago and have never needed them since. To some extent, other exercises can also help in the same way, like stretching, calisthenics, weight training and swimming. So the healthy hedonist gets a double lift from working out regularly: fitness and some of the fine effects of bodywork.

13

The Beauty Quest

The pleasure philosopher is always seeking new ways to enjoy himself. Because of this, he becomes quite sensitive to his surroundings and environment. He realizes that pleasure is more than just intense sensation, that there are subtle, refined pleasures as well. The bliss-seeker understands that what you constantly see around you affects your inner sensibilities. If you're always exposed to dirt, disorder and degradation, it'll be pretty tough to maintain a placid, unperturbed state of mind. On the other hand, continued exposure to objects of beauty will help create a tranquil, serene mood.

So, the pleasure philosopher does whatever he can to put himself in a pleasing, aesthetic environment. Whenever possible, he'll avoid scenes involving pain, anger or negativity. For example, if he passes an accident while driving, he won't pull over to gape, unless he's stopping to assist. Similarly, he won't become addicted to the sensational, often gory details of crime stories, gossip columns and front-page headlines. He's not trying to blind himself to reality, but is simply choosing to focus on its more positive aspects. He appreciates the computer operators' edict, "garbage in, garbage out," and limits his intake of junk accordingly. He tries to replace negative conditions with positive, uplifting influences. This is what the Beauty Quest is all about.

There are many aspects to this quest. On a material level, the bliss-seeker always endeavors to fill his settings with as much beauty as he can. If his budget permits, he may invest in fine objects of art, handsome furnishings and intricate interior decorating. Avant-garde sensualists may install hot tubs, Jacuzzis, saunas, multimedia light shows, projector TVs and the like. The materially well-off bliss-seeker will also put together a tasteful wardrobe, consisting of the finest fabrics. He'll dress in well-coordinated color combinations and will make his clothing choices suit the shape of his frame. On the other hand, those with tighter budgets are by no means precluded from a successful beauty quest. Only a few things are essential for a pleasant personal setting: comfort, neatness and cleanliness. Even a spartan setup can be satisfying if everything available is comfy, simple and clean.

The lower-budget sensualist simply has to be more discerning in his selections. He must experiment and shop around for bargains among lesser-known but equally satisfying products. The same goes for clothing. It's possible to look elegant on all occasions with a small wardrobe of quality items which can be mixed and matched.

The key to the beauty quest, regardless of wallet size, is a discerning eye. The thoughtful bliss-seeker tries to develop aesthetic sensibilities to guide his choices. He may study art, music or philosophy, or simply nourish his innate feelings about the nature of beauty. He'll keep close watch on his creative urges, because they'll lead him in aesthetic appreciation. He may express himself through crafts and hobbies like photography, painting, woodwork, etchings, etc. This will allow him to produce his own objects of beauty, which will be a continual source of inspiration. He can also explore other modes of expression like gourmet cooking, collecting and music appreciation. Books and courses abound where one can learn about pursuits of all sorts.

The pleasure philosopher will find that his beauty quest will be amply appreciated by others. These times of mass-market entertainment give people less opportunity to express the unique aspects of their inner selves. They get caught up in the same best-selling novels and shows that everyone else is caught up in, which creates a boring sameness in their dialogue. Someone with refined, individual sensitivities will be seen as interesting and intriguing. He can teach you something unique, rather than just repeat what everyone else is into. He'll usually be in great demand as an acquaintance, friend or lover. And since his nurtured sense of beauty will reflect itself in his surroundings, people will be glad to spend time at his place.

The beauty quest also includes a profound appreciation for both natural and man-made wonders of the world. The bliss-seeker almost always puts a high value on travel, for he understands that it develops one's tastes, broadens one's horizons and leads to self-transcendence. He'll be intrigued by the possibility of seeing new cultures and new lifestyles, marveling at the sight of scenic wonders. He also realizes the value of vacations for restoring spent energies, allaying burnout and removing one from the daily grind. Once again, the key to creative travel is not big bucks, but sensible discrimination. Shopping around for best prices, traveling off-season, and exploring group charters and package deals are all ways to stretch one's vacation budget.

The beauty-seeker will not allow his travel decisions to be dictated by mass marketing. He's likely not to want to flock where all the other vacation sheep are heading, but to pick offbeat places not flooded by tourists. Or he may visit popular spots during the off season and get the best of local culture. He may also choose recreation spots purely for their isolation and natural beauty. The romantic in him will thrill to the idea of a secluded beach, private cabin, out-of-the-way resort. And he may find such places close by home, allowing him to save considerable travel time and money. Almost all states have beautiful vacation areas way off the beaten path: lakes, hills, campgrounds, parks, shores, etc. You can usually learn about them by writing to the Departments of Tourism or Commerce in the states in your vicinity.

Coming up with inventive, original travel destinations will also enhance your reputation with others. You may find yourself being tapped as a tour guide to offbeat, little-known spots in your area. Of course, an ideal choice for a travel companion is an intimate pleasure partner. There's probably nothing more romantic than walking hand in hand with a lover at some scenic splendor. A majestic natural setting can lend an incredibly lusty air to your pleasure explorations. Sleeping under the stars, making love on a secluded beach, strolling in a moonlit forest are all excellent ways of adding fire to the flames of your affair.

Whatever your individual inclinations in the realm of beauty, it pays to nurture and nourish them. The first step is simply to open your eyes wide and appreciate the myriad magical marvels that surround you. Too often, we get hypnotized and lulled by the dictates of mass marketing. It's much healthier to look at the world through the innocent, wonder-struck eyes of a child. The youngster sees the sky and wonders why it's blue, while most adults hardly notice the sky at all! Tear the filter of mass culture off and you'll start to view things as they really are. Then you can go out and embrace the unlimited beauties just waiting for your attention!

This natural, spontaneous, childlike wonder can also be fostered by simply allowing yourself to be silly. Unfortunately, we enclose ourselves in social roles and masks marked by seriousness, soberness and "sensibility." And while they may be effective for dealing with the superficialities of daily life, they hinder our aesthetic abilities. We *become* the roles and masks without realizing it. Is it any great mystery why our capacity to experience pure joy and exultation has been greatly limited? Our culture tries to fill the gaps with artificial distractions like stale comedians, ridiculous sitcoms and canned laughter. But it doesn't work. You can't manufacture genuine humor in a machine shop or on Madison Avenue. Our inner selves ache for real joy, whether we consciously realize it or not.

So the beauty quest involves going past the social niceties to let your hair down. There are several ways to find out if you're unconsciously controlled by cultural norms. Ask yourself a few telling questions. If you're a man, do you shave each morning regardless of whether you'll be seeing anyone that day? For both sexes, do you use deodorant even if you'll only be staying home alone? Do you lock the bathroom door even when no one else is around? Positive answers to these and

similar questions show that you may be unthinkingly carrying out social norms round the clock. But these rituals are exactly what must be transcended in order to once again experience childlike sensibilities.

The childlike perception assures you of a world filled with mystery, magic and awe. Each leaf falling, squirrel scampering or cat scurrying will seem special. You'll be especially sensitive to natural splendors like sunsets, sunrises and waterfalls, which will fill you with majesty, harmony and spiritual insight. One thing for sure: You'll no longer take anything for granted. Peel away the stereotyped, clouded layers of social conditioning and you'll find that everything is filled with poignant significance. Many of the "primitive" peoples of the world retain this capacity, mainly because they've never been through the rigid filters of our social order. Tribal peoples from South America, Africa, Australia and other places feel no separation between themselves and nature. They feel interconnected with the universe, in sharp contrast to modern man's alienated, isolated orientation. Tribal societies keep close to the rhythms of nature, and see spiritual presences in all things. Philosophers may dismiss this as naive pantheism, but some of the most sophisticated religious systems see things exactly the same way.

For example, Buddhism, Hinduism and Taoism all view God as immanent in all, existing in all forms and appearances. Even inert minerals contact a spark of divine energy. From this perspective, everything is seen as sacred, permeated with God's power and essence. This leads to a respect for all life, an awareness of unity with all and a desire to preserve and revere the environment. Many people active in the ecology movement share this awareness. They appreciate and respect the beauty of nature's creations in much the same way that the spontaneous, untainted child does. The goal of many spiritual traditions is to rediscover our original childhood innocence. As Christ said, "Ye must be as little children to enter the kingdom of God."

Christ also indicated that the Kingdom of God lies within. If you combine both statements, then the key to the divine spark within is the return to childlike innocence. In essence, this means unlocking the beauty inside you, a beauty just as wonderful as any external phenomena. In fact, some spiritual traditions hold that the world will be beautiful and nurturing in exact proportion to the inner beauty you allow to unfold. For instance, the popular "Course in Miracles" study program teaches that the external is really a reflection of your inner state of mind. If you harbor angry, hateful or fearful thoughts, your world will be filled with angry, hateful and fearful experiences. Conversely, filling your mind with loving, helpful, caring thoughts will result in similar outer experiences. We'll explore these spiritual insights in greater detail in a later chapter.

So the Beauty Quest is a journey within, as well as without. Tear off the facades of artificial social conventions; liberate yourself from destructive, binding thinking; don't dwell on ugliness and violence; and you'll make great strides on the road to beauty. Get out and appreciate nature's wonders, meditate on inspiring, uplifting thoughts and allow the suppressed child inside free expression. Drop the deadly serious approach to life and relax enough to enjoy fun, games and pure playtime. You have nothing to lose, and plenty to gain. If the world is headed for destruction anyway, as so many doomsayers predict, your fretting and worrying about it is not going to make one whit of difference. You might as well put aside the world's woes and enjoy yourself while you can. Spread sunshine wherever you go and you'll find it reflected back at you.

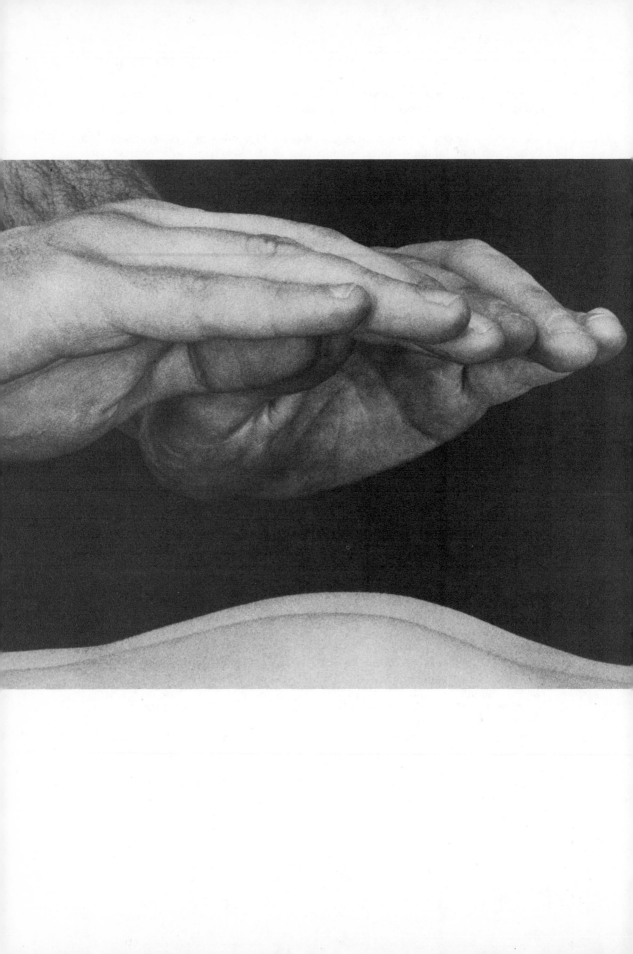

14

Psychic Pleasure

Up until this point we've discussed tangible ecstasies like love, sensuality and sex. But there are also more subtle, elusive pleasures that can enlarge your capacity for enjoyment in other areas. These pleasures help you transcend reality because they affect the psychic and spiritual centers of your body. They empower these centers, making you more effective in your daily efforts. They help rid the system of deeply engrained psychic blockages, impacted areas in the emotions and thoughts which have been built up since childhood. They have a healing, calming, restorative effect. The techniques are also quite enjoyable in themselves, leading to profound relaxation and inner peace.

Psychic pleasure methods derive from ancient sources and traditions, including both Eastern and Western spiritual sources. Modern science casts some light on why they work, though it can't explain the whole picture. Various scientific experiments point to the existence of an energy field which surrounds the body. This field emanates from the physical body itself, surrounding it on all sides. A special type of electromagnetic photography called "Kirlian" photography has produced pictures of what appears to be such a field. Soviet scientists have labeled this the "bioplasma body."

Kirlian shots have shown that sick people have broken, weak energy fields, while psychic healers have powerful, full fields. When a healer works on a sick person, Kirlian work reveals that the healer's field is reduced, while the sick person's is enhanced. This probably reflects a direct energy transfer from healer to patient. Other experiments show evidence of electromagnetic energies around the body. Voltmeters attached to different body parts show negative magnetic charges in some spots, and positive charges in others. These experiments seem to show that there's much more to the body than meets the eye.

Ancient mystical and occult traditions talk about the "aura," an energy emanation which quite neatly fits the description of the modern "energy field" or "bioplasma body." Many current occultists feel that science is finally catching up with their teachings. But the mystics go well beyond what science has been able to establish. Some occultists, joined by certain Soviet scientists, consider the aura to be the "true" or primary body, while the physical self is simply a dense crystallization of this energy field. Both ancient Hindu philosophy (yoga) and medieval Western magical tradition describe special energy centers in the auric body. These centers are special focal points for healing and power. Yogis call them "chakras" (wheels).

The chakras have counterpoints in the physical frame, located along the spinal column and head. By working on these physical centers, you also affect the aura. Certain difficult life experiences cause the chakras to become blocked, resulting in both physical and emotional disorders. Clearing up these blockages releases trapped tensions, removes repressed feelings and liberates stagnant energies. At the same time, deep-rooted psychological conflicts may become more evident and in some cases be lessened or even resolved. Each chakra has a special affinity with some area of experience. When you unblock a given chakra, you also unclog the area of experience associated with it. Repressed memories may surface; long-suppressed emotions may come into consciousness. The rewards can be enormous. You'll no longer be wasting energy holding down forbidden feelings.

"Chakra cleansing" is the yoga term for our first psychic pleasure technique. There are seven chakras in this system, each with a different significance. The first chakra is located along the base of the spine, and is associated with survival and security. Your central attitudes toward your right to exist will get centered in this "root" chakra (that is, how "grounded" you feel). The next chakra is on the spine, parallel to the genitals, and governs sexuality and sensuality. Blockages here refer to sexual inhibitions.

The third chakra lines up with the navel area along the spine. This represents your feelings toward power and will. Blockages here mean restrictions on your ability to express power and will. The fourth spinal chakra is at the level of the heart. This "heart center" is connected with your ability to love and to receive. The fifth spinal chakra is parallel with the throat, and stands for your ability to express yourself. Childhood prohibitions on self-expression ("children should be seen but not heard") get reflected as blockages here. The sixth chakra is located between the eyebrows and is known as the "third eye center." It refers to "psychic sight," the ability to see beyond surface appearances. The seventh chakra is at the crown of the head and represents spiritual awareness, your connection with transcendent, metaphysical manifestations, like awareness of higher spiritual beings.

The chakra cleansing technique is a very simple meditation which can be performed in ten minutes or so. It will help open up all the centers, ridding you of the blockages which restrict and constrain you. This meditation can also be used as a regular tool for relaxation and restoration, as discussed before in the section on meditation. You can read the instructions, then follow them, or tape them and play them back. Soft, gentle music can enhance the mood. The following technique has been given high praise by students I use it with in my classes. It has been derived from teachings of several spiritual masters. Preliminaries: Sit with your back straight on a chair in total darkness or in soft, indirect lighting. Relax, breathe deeply and close your eyes. Just remain silent for a short time before starting.

Let your mind go on an expansive journey to the cosmos. Envision outer space, and look for a natural source of brilliant light. This can be any source you feel comfortable with: the sun, stars, moon, planets, comets, asteroids, etc. See a brilliant beam of pure white light streaming from this source toward the earth. See it enter the atmosphere and head for your area. Envision this beautiful cleansing white light penetrating the walls of your dwelling and heading straight for the crown on top of your head. View the crown of your head as a flower opening up its petals to receive the cosmic embrace of this life-sustaining, healing white light.

Now feel the light penetrate your crown and pulsate all the way down to your spine. See it collect itself at the base of your spine into a glowing, hot white ball of light, like a miniature sun. Feel this potent fiery light opening your root chakra, allowing you to release any restrictions you harbor about your right to exist. Let the light work on this center for two minutes or so. Then see it move up to your spinal area parallel to your genitals. Feel it open up your sex center, burning away all sexual and sensual inhibitions. Continue this cleansing process for two minutes or so. Now move further up the spine to the navel area. Sense the brilliant ball of

THE PLEASURE BOOK

light opening this will center, loosening all blockages about expressing and manifesting your power in the world. Stay with this cleansing a few minutes.

Then envision the blazing white light moving up parallel with your heart, removing and eliminating all restrictions in the flow of love and receiving. Continue this healing for two minutes, then move the light up to the throat center. Feel it blazing away all prohibitions on self-expression, eliminating all old influences against speaking freely. You can now express yourself clearly, easily and forcefully, if needed. Stay with this cleansing for a few minutes, then feel the light ball move up to the area between your eyebrows. Let the light cleanse your psychic sight center, clearing your inner vision so you can separate truth from surface appearances. Continue this cleansing for several minutes.

Then let the light move up to the crown of your head, where it will open up your spiritual center, linking you with transcendent, mystical power. If you believe in God or a higher spiritual power, this is the time to make contact with it. Stay with this process for several minutes, then allow the light slowly to recede from your crown. As it recedes, feel it pulling all negative feelings along with it—sickness, pain, anger, envy, resentment, distress, despair—any problem that's plaguing you on any level, psychological, physical, emotional, etc. See yourself surrendering all these negatives to the light—rather like tossing them into a cosmic furnace—as the light pulls them to it like an irresistible, giant magnet. Then envision the light burning away these problems as it streams back to its cosmic source. Feel the light returning to its stellar origin, taking your problems along with it to be further burned away in space, as your crown center slowly closes its flowerlike petals. See these petals stay open a bit, so you always maintain some receptivity to this transcendent, cosmic light.

Now feel yourself gradually returning to normal awareness. When you feel ready, open your eyes and if you were in darkness, turn the lights back on. You'll feel renewed, refreshed, and energized. White light has been chosen for this meditation because of its clean, purifying associations. However, each chakra has a special healing color associated with it, and you can vary this meditation by using these colors. At the point where the white light has reached the base of the spine, envision it changing into the root center color, a bright red. When the light reaches the sex center, it changes to a brilliant orange. And so on for the other chakras: yellow for the will center, green for the heart, blue for the throat, indigo for the third eye and violet for the crown. As the light leaves your body, see it changing back to pure white. If you tape these instructions, simply substitute the respective colors for the white light in the original exercise. But whatever version you use, the results should be equally beneficial. While each center has a special color connected with it, white light serves as a general healing influence.

You can also perform these exercises with a partner, who can read the instructions to you. However, you can work even more effectively with a partner utilizing a second psychic pleasure technique. This is a simple healing tool derived from the ancient practice called "laying on of hands." Modern versions are now taught as part of graduate programs in nursing, and have been used effectively in hospital settings. Studies have shown that it leads to profound relaxation and pain reduction. We're now going to combine this ancient technique with the chakra cleansing already described.

The idea is to pass your hands over the front of the body of your partner at the level of each chakra. Your hands should be side by side, either resting lightly on your friend's body or *over* it about six inches (so you can work directly on the energy field or aura). Start with your hands near the root chakra center (near the base of the spine) and feel the energy pouring out of your hands to your friend's body. You may feel a sensation of heat flow from your hands to the body. (You can test this energy at another time by holding your palms face-to-face and slowly moving them back and forth, closer and further apart. You'll eventually notice a tingling or warmth radiate between them; this is the healing energy used on the chakras.) Keep this energy flow going for a few minutes. Then move up to the next center, near the genitals. Repeat this movement for all the remaining chakras.

You can also use this energy flow to help out with specific body ailments or pain. Place your left palm on one side of an afflicted area in your friend's body, and your right palm on the other side. Feel the energy streaming into the painful part. The flow between your palms forms a balanced energy circuit which can help reduce pain and release blockages in both the chakras and any other spot. You and your partner can share these techniques with each other, alternating the giving and receiving roles. The methods take little effort and energy and can be approached in an exploratory, fun way. Since both chakra cleansing and psychic healing contribute to calmness, sensitivity and relaxation, they can be excellent preludes to sensual involvements. They can also be comfortably combined with many of the other pleasure techniques described in this book. Find a favorite pleasure partner and give them a try!

15

Spiritual Pleasure

To most minds, spiritual expression and pleasure simply don't mix. They are put in totally separate domains. We normally associate spirituality with otherworldly concerns: God, heaven, unseen forces, faith, etc. Pleasure, on the other hand, seems much more earthbound: sex, sensualism, fun, play, etc. But actually, the separation is more apparent than real. We've already shown some of the connections in the chapter on psychic pleasure. We demonstrated that chakra cleansing and psychic healing—two spiritual practices—can be used to remove blocks and inhibitions and thus boost one's pleasure capacities. We've also made other strong links between pleasure and brotherly love, meditation, the search for beauty and social concerns, all spiritual pursuits in their own right.

In reality, spirituality may be one of the most refined forms of pleasure available, as well as one of the most intense. The ultimate goal of spirituality is union with the source of being, whether you call it God, Allah, Atman, Brahma, the universal life force or anything else. This is the profound experience the mystics call "cosmic consciousness." The terms used to describe it certainly belong in anyone's pleasure vocabulary—ecstasy, absolute awareness, bliss, mystical merger, etc. One point should be made clear: We're not talking about your everyday Sunday church service. While it is possible to receive inspiration and some degree of spiritual enlightenment in such settings, the mystical experience has typically taken place outside the confines of organized religion.

Unfortunately, traditional religions have tended to rigidify and lose much of the fire infused by the masters who founded them. Sunday services often become reduced to empty rituals and platitudes from the pulpit, after which you return to the rat-race reality of football games and the daily grind. Mystical revelations are not limited to a few short hours a week, but permeate one's entire perspective. They transform your world view, change your values and have a profound, intense effect on the core of your being. This is one of the reasons they can be so useful to the pleasure-seeker. Peak experiences are one of his goals, and mysticism rates high on the scale. There are even further links between spirituality and pleasure. For example, the chapter on mental pleasure presented methods for replacing negative thinking with positive thinking. This is really a practice with deep spiritual roots.

Remember, the classic *The Power of Positive Thinking* was written by a minister, the Reverend Norman Vincent Peale. Similar books, like the *Magic of Believing* and the *Magic of Thinking Big,* are from the same spiritual tradition. James Allen's classic *As A Man Thinketh* sums up the spiritual basis for positive thinking: What you really believe in your heart will eventually come to pass in your life. This is where faith, visualization and prayer come in. Negative sentiments like doubt, fear and worry are really the reverse of this process. Worry and fear attract the very conditions you seek to avoid, so it's crucial to keep away from them at all costs. Override them by feeding your mind with positive, uplifting thoughts, implanting in your subconscious the outcomes you really want to attain.

And what if you happen to be an atheist or agnostic? This does not render spiritual practices irrelevant, because there's a way of seeing the whole process from a purely secular perspective. If you don't believe in God, you can still use the techniques from a psychological viewpoint. Perhaps the best statement of this is in Maxwell Maltz's *Psychocybernetics.* Maltz portrays the subconscious mind as an automatic goal-seeking mechanism, sort of like a guided missile. Whatever direction you point it at, it moves toward that goal. The missile itself has no goals, but its targets are implanted from other sources. In the case of the subconscious, the conscious mind can be used to plant goals with positive thinking, suggestion and imaging. Then the subconscious, like a servomechanism, carries out the instructions without question.

Therefore, you needn't be a "believer" in a religious sense to gain from spiritual practices. However, the most benefit can be gained when one does have faith in a higher power. The psychocybernetics approach is useful, but it only takes you so far. More sophisticated systems divide the mind not only into conscious and subconscious, but *superconscious* as well. The superconscious represents Universal Mind or God, and is linked to the conscious by the subconscious. While the psychocybernetics approach plants thoughts from the conscious to the subconscious, higher spiritual practices like meditation make direct contact with the superconscious. As Eric Butterworth, minister of New York's branch of Unity Church, explains, meditation allows messages from the superconscious or God-self to seep into awareness. By "going into the silence," as many traditions call it, you can gain valuable information about your mission, goals, ends, etc.

So meditation can be seen as God speaking to you. Prayer, on the other hand, is when your conscious mind addresses God. Unfortunately, most modern prayer is negative, which is why it rarely seems to be answered. Conventional prayer involves a supplicant attitude in which you ask or even beg a supreme being to do something for you. This is usually combined with a degrading humility taught by so many conventional religious dogmas. As Reverend Ike, the New York "prosperity consciousness" minister puts it, conventional dogma makes us feel evil, sinful and unworthy of blessings. Reverend Ike likes to cite a particularly dangerous prayer hymn which includes the words "for such a worm as I." With such a negative self-image being put forth, is it any wonder prayers go unanswered? As Reverend Ike graphically asserts, "What happens to worms? *They get stepped on.*"

James Allen, in his tape *Secrets of Success,* says the right attitude toward prayer should be to see oneself as a child of God fully deserving of His bounties. Instead of lowly worms, Allen says we should pray with the attitude that we "are of *royal* blood." There is certainly plenty of biblical support for the views of the Reverends Butterworth, Ike and James Allen. You'll find constant references to the power of faith and belief. Jesus said that faith could heal, and belief could move mountains. Prayer, in summary, should not be begging God for something. Instead, you should fully believe you deserve what you want, and you should phrase your prayers in positive, affirmative statements, much like the positive affirmations described in chapter 5. Mystics teach that there's tremendous power attached to any words following the assertion "I AM." (Remember, God in the burning bush told Moses that his name was I AM THAT I AM.) In my own daily prayer affirmations, I silently, confidently repeat phrases like "I AM peace, power, plenty, presence, patience, tolerance, love, wisdom, success, prosperity, affluence, abundance, opulence."

While doing this, I see my body bathed in white or violent healing light. If I want specific things to happen in my life, as opposed to general qualities, I affirm, "and I manifest in my life now . . ." whatever material conditions I desire, at the same time envisioning them happening. Desire is a crucial element here. Hindu cosmology holds that we're surrounded by several sheaths of increasingly fine substance. The densest is the physical. Then there's the astral, which is the seat of emotions and desires. The next sheath is the "causal body," the realm of pure thought and ideas. According to the Hindus, the way to make anything manifest on the material level is to firmly plant the thought of the desired condition in the mind (causal plane), and infuse it with burning, consuming desire (astral plane). The speed of manifestation depends upon the intensity of your desire, the tenacity of your thoughts, as well as your state of spiritual advancement. Yogi saints described in Yogananda's *Autobiography of a Yogi* were said to produce food out of thin air. Moses parted the Red Sea and Jesus turned water into wine. But whether you're a Master or ordinary person, the process is the same, it just takes longer.

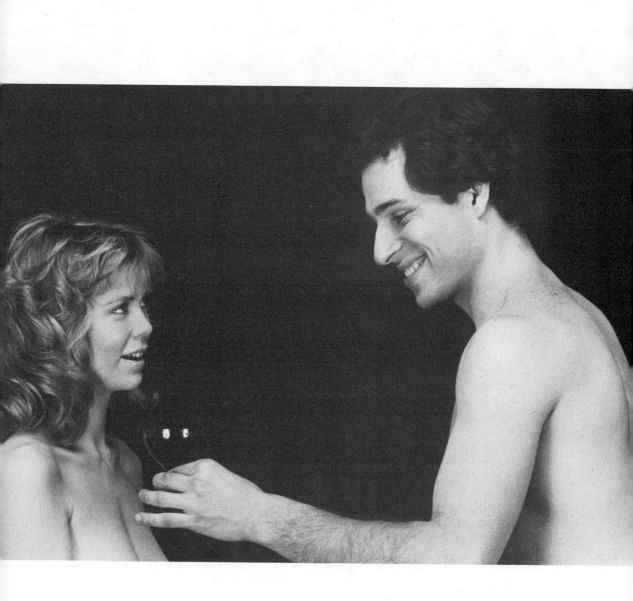

110

You must also guard against creeping disbelief, since lack of faith will ruin prayer. Even if your prayers appear to go unanswered for some time, don't let discouragement set in. It could be that what you consciously desire is not really best for your present state of evolution, but that something even better is on the way. For example, you may be praying for a Toyota, while the Universe may be ready to send a Mercedes your way. Don't get hung up on results; just keep praying and express gratitude that your prayers have already been answered (another mystical law holds that being grateful always multiplies your good). Firmly feel that "it is done" and go about your business, confident that your desires will indeed come to pass, although in ways that may amaze you.

And how do these spiritual practices increase your pleasure? The connection should be quite clear. By using prayer properly, you can literally bring about your fondest fantasies, keenest desires, greatest needs. If the scriptures and spiritual Masters are correct, the power of prayer and faith can bring about any condition you want, as long as it's not harmful to others or your own inner development. Do you have a pet pleasure that's been eluding you for some time? Try ardently praying, affirming and believing that it'll come to pass. Don't worry about the "hows"; let the Universe take care of that. You may be pleasantly surprised at the results.

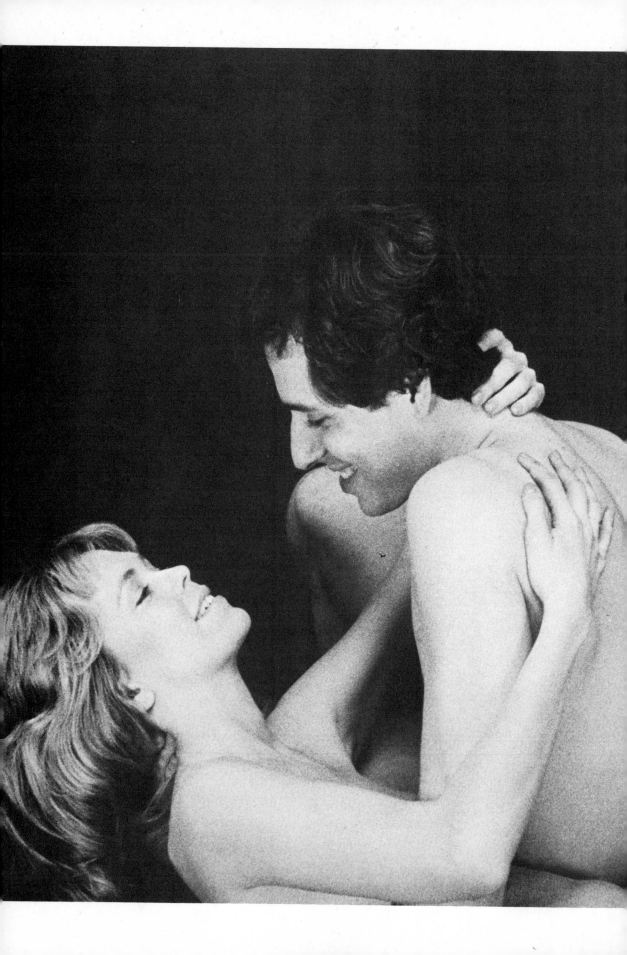

16

Sensual Pleasure—
Touch

Loving touch is a supreme pleasure experience. Unfortunately, most people limit intense touching to sexuality. Fact is, touch is an independent biological drive which can't be sated by sex alone. We continually need a great deal of skin stimulation for optimum health and well-being. Study after study has shown that touch deprivation can lead to serious psychological and physical disorders, including the loss of the body's ability to ward off disease. While sexual contact helps—it's clearly far better than nothing—erotic touching is too random and disorganized to fully satisfy our skin hunger. What's needed is a systematic, sustained type of skin arousal.

There are many ways to scratch the human touch itch, some of which can be done alone. For example, clothes tend to restrict the skin, so it helps to do without clothes whenever alone. The skin thrives on contact with the air, which allows it to breathe freely. Spending time unclad on the beach (or with minimum bathing wear) with open exposure to sea breezes, sun and sand is an excellent way to satisfy this need. Immersion in water is also beneficial, whether it be surf, shower, pool, hot tub or the old-fashioned bath. Walks in the woods, jogging by the shore, or outdoor sports like tennis or basketball are also solid ways of getting needed skin strokes. But you can just go so far with solitary activities. The real heart of all touch action comes through contact with others.

It makes sense to obtain as much tactile involvement as you can. There are actually therapists who prescribe "hugs for health," with a minimum maintenance dosage being four a day. Of course, you can't hug everyone you deal with, but there are some satisfying substitutes. Stroking pets, for example, is highly gratifying for the skin. Studies show that touching pets reduces tension by lowering the pulse and heart rate, and may actually ward off heart disease! Apart from pets, most pleasure-seekers surround themselves with people who love to hug and caress. This is especially important for your primary pleasure partner, who'll be sharing the most intimate embraces with you. If he or she is afraid to touch, you'll be in for some cold nights.

While it's always good to share plenty of hugs with close friends, there's a simple way to obtain virtually all the touching you need in one session. This is through a technique I call the "sensuous art of cuddling." Creative cuddling entails being fully nude in bed with your friend. The full cuddling cycle can involve around a dozen positions, and you can get the total picture in my *Joy of Touch* chapter on the topic. For our purposes, all we need to indicate is that cuddling allows you and your partner to rub every area of your bodies together. Some of the key positions include face-to-face, back-to-face (the popular "spoon position"), back-to-back and one partner lying over the other.

THE PLEASURE BOOK

All cuddling positions maximize contact by embracing, wrapping limbs around each other, and snuggling bodies up close. By varying postures, every inch of your skin will eventually be stroked. You just hold each position until you feel satisfied, then move on to the next. This leads to profound relaxation, and it can also be highly stimulating. Before sex, cuddling can serve as a sort of foreplay. An ideal situation is to start a sexual encounter with cuddling, move to explicit foreplay and sex itself, then waft off onto exquisite relaxation after sex with another round of sensual snuggling. You'll find this a treat that's hard to beat! You can then either drift off into blissful sleep, or continue to cuddle till you warm up for another erotic encounter.

Practice cuddling regularly with a close pleasure partner and you'll see a special bond build between you. So much warmth, nurturance and caring gets exchanged that you develop a special intimacy called a "cuddle bond," a closeness that transcends both sex and love. Your bodies become a tightly knit pair. Even fully clothed and in public, you'll probably share more kisses, caresses and plain-old shoulder rubbing than the noncuddling couple. Cuddling can be considered the "lazy person's sensuality" because you're simply bathing in the luxury of each

other's bodies, just nuzzling and heaping together like young pups. But there's an equally tempting touch treat that requires a bit more effort: sensual massage.

Many people feel that massage requires a great deal of expertise and technical skill. Indeed, it is possible to spend two years studying for a massage license. You can learn the special strokes of Swedish massage, anatomy, physiology and other related subjects. But you really don't need such elaborate training to give a good massage. Intuition and common sense are just as important as technical background. Massage really boils down to stroking someone's entire body in a loving way. The body can be broken down into large-, small- and medium-sized muscle areas. Likewise, your hands also contain large- (palms), small- (fingertips and thumbs) and medium-sized areas (flats of the fingers). A very simple massage formula is to fit your hands to the muscles you're working on. For example, large muscles like the buttocks and thighs can be worked with the palms, mid-size sections like the arms with the full fingers and delicate spots like the face with the fingertips.

Of course, you may want more instruction than this simple guideline, so we'll be describing a short guide to a full-body sensual massage. But before doing that, some important preliminaries should be noted. While it's possible to give a sensual massage on a bed without oil, the best experience will be had by using a natural, vegetable-based oil (which can be scented with spearmint, peppermint essences, etc.) and a massage table (alternatively, a well-cushioned floor). Oil allows your hands to glide easily, permitting deep rubbing. Use sheets underneath your friend to sop up excess oil. A massage table permits balance and ease of movement, while a bed will tire you out in no time. Once you've picked an oil (spills can be avoided by using a plastic squeeze bottle) and obtained a suitable setting (the floor being a compromise between table and bed), the next consideration is creating a sensual, relaxed mood.

This can include soft music, comfortable lighting, incense, or whatever you think will enhance the experience. The room should be warm, free from drafts, and you should make sure no distractions or interruptions will ensue. Your partner should be fully nude, and you may also want to be as well. Let him or her decide whether you should begin on the front or back first. If there's no preference, it's usually best to start on the back, because many people feel vulnerable when you work on the front first. Doing the back will allow you to relax and loosen the person for more intimate contact later.

Have your partner lie comfortably on his or her stomach, arms at sides. Position yourself behind the head. Before all moves, rub oil onto your palms. An excellent opening move is long strokes down the side of the body, starting at the shoulders and continuing to the hips. Do both sides at once and repeat this movement, like all subsequent ones, two or three times. Then knead the shoulder muscles and neck. Wipe the oil off your hands before rubbing the scalp vigorously with fingertips (hairy areas should not have oil applied to them). Put more oil on your palms, then move over to the left side of your friend's body and massage all the muscles on the left back, getting under the shoulder blades, along the spine, around the hips, etc. Move to the right side and do the same areas there. Then inch down to the buttocks, kneading and vibrating them vigorously. From there, work down to the backs of the thighs, which also enjoy solid pressure. Proceed down the leg to the calves, using moderate pressure on the knotty calf muscles, then to the Achilles tendon and rear of the foot. Finish the back with long, gliding strokes from feet to hips.

Now have your friend turn over. Maintain your position by his feet, and begin the front of the body with long, gliding strokes from feet to upper thighs. Then thoroughly massage each foot, taking care to knead all muscles and bones there. Knead up the top of the foot past the shins, lightening the pressure at the knees, but renewing it on the large muscles of the thighs. Deeply knead and press the thighs all over, then continue on the hip and pelvic areas. If you like, and your partner is prepared for it, you can also massage the genitals. The female vagina should be rubbed delicately and lightly, while the male organ can stand more pressure. Some lovers like to alternate explicit sexual strokes, such as oral stimulation, with massage movements. Just be sure to remove all oil before beginning.

The next move is abdomen kneading, using relatively moderate pressure. Massage this area in a clockwise fashion from left to right, following the contours of the colon. From there, work on the chest, with lighter pressure for the female breasts, and deeper pressure for male chest muscles. You can also try sexual stimulation of the nipples of both sexes. The next step is the shoulder area, then the arms. Do each arm at a time, propping it up on your thigh for balance. Knead and press the entire arm using both hands. Then massage each hand, getting deep into the tissues with your fingertips and thumbs.

Next, perform light massage movements on the delicate neck tissues, then gently cover the entire face with fingertip strokes. You'll want to be especially sensitive with the face, paying special attention to the lips, cheeks, around the eyes, forehead and ears. Some lovers like to add soft kisses to sensual spots like the mouth and ears. When the face has been finished, give the scalp some more vigorous rubbing (remember, no oil on hair), then complete the massage with long, gliding strokes from the shoulders to the hips. Gradually, imperceptibly, lighten the strokes until you're barely brushing the skin, then remove your hands entirely. At this point, it's important just to let your friend lie quietly, perhaps covering him or her with a sheet for warmth. Your friend will be wafting gently in a wonderful world of blissful sensations, and you don't want to disturb him or her too soon.

After fifteen minutes or so, help him or her up to a sitting position, unless your friend is asleep, in which case just let him or her be.

You have several options once your partner has stirred. If you've agreed to swap massages, it's now your turn to enjoy yourself. Or you can lead your lover to the bathroom and continue to pamper him or her with a bath or shower to remove excess oil. You can share the bath or shower and then you can both towel, powder and perfume each other up. Your next stop can easily be the comfortable confines of the bedroom, where you can continue your sensual explorations with cuddling or erotic activity. To your delight, you'll discover that massage is a perfect aid to relaxation, releasing tension and loosening your body to the point of peak sexual receptivity. Sensual massage is a perfect prelude to sexual exploration, especially with people who are somewhat prone to inhibitions.

Another touch technique for breaking inhibitions is old-fashioned tickling. It can be used as a fun game, to generate excitement, and to loosen up an otherwise uptight partner. There's a special "tickle stroke" that can literally drive someone up the wall. It consists of feathery light movements with the fingers in a circular, twirling fashion. Tickling makes the body all tingly and goosebumpy, so it's a perfect complement to any other erotic explorations. Different areas of the body have differing sensitivities to it. Top spots include the pubic area, tummy, thighs and knees. Nearly as receptive are the buttocks, soles of the feet and underarms. Certain areas like the erogenous zones are clearly sensitive to both tickling and erotic sensations.

Each person, of course, varies in tickling responsiveness, so you may have to explore a bit before finding your partner's irresistible areas. The truly great thing about tickling is its versatility. It can be employed for simple sensual enjoyment, or as serious sex therapy. Let's say you're hooked up with someone who can't relax in bed. Perhaps you're a man with a woman who seemingly can't reach climax no matter what you do. Without even indicating your intentions are sexual, you can start playfully tickling her in nonerotic areas. She'll figure you're just into having fun, and you may end up in a "tickle match" to see who can handle it best. This can even develop into a hot and heavy "tickle wrestling" match in which each of you tries to pin the other's hands down (using your body), leaving one of you free to tickle the other into submission.

This wrestling match can be quite stimulating by itself, and after one of you submits, you may find you're both ready for sex. But even without the contest, you can eroticize things markedly by moving to increasingly erotic tickling. Go from the tummy and navel areas right to the nipples and the "V" lines emanating from the pubic area. With women, you can even try tickling the clitoris and outside the vaginal lips. Do this with skill and you'll find that a lot of your friend's inhibitions will have melted away. To put the action at an even more feverish pace, try alternating tickling movements with direct erotic stimulation. For example, men can switch from tickling the tummy or pubis to oral-clitoral contact. Slowly go back and forth between these activities and you'll find her moving closer and closer to climax. Tickling and erotic play can be an unbeatable orgasmic combination.

But even if you're not into tickling, you can still loosen up an uptight lover by ordinary play-wrestling. Without using too much force, just lock up your bodies together, tumbling all around, trying to see who can make the other one yell "uncle" first. The stronger partner should not use all his might, because the object is not victory, but stimulation. Actually, losing can be just as arousing as winning. Being pinned by a sexy partner can be quite a sensual experience. But if active games like tickling and wrestling aren't appropriate—perhaps your friend is

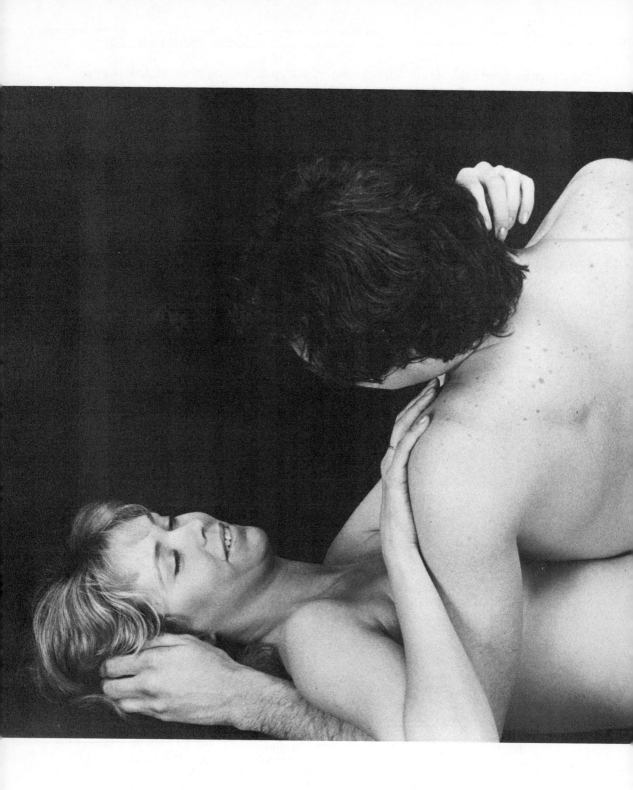

118

scared or withdrawn—another tactic is to simply hold him or her in a secure, nurturing embrace. You can use the cuddle positions to do this, or simply a natural, mothering hold that will make him or her feel loved, wanted and appreciated. This can build trust, concern and caring, which may have been the missing ingredients in your sex play, especially with new partners. Uptightness in both sexes can often be traced to fear of the unknown—"Just who is this person?"—and reassuring, nonpressured gestures can be quite helpful here.

There are still other ways to titillate through touch. A large feather, boa or swatch of fur can be run along your friend's body for added bliss. Long-haired women can run their sensuous locks over their men's bodies for a similar sensual delight. Another sensuous treat is to bring a well-trained pet into bed with you. You can pass a soft animal around between you—cats are perfect for this— snuggling against its silky fur. But perhaps the ultimate way of sharing touch bliss is the hot new trend, hydromassage devices. From California hot tubs to East Coast Jacuzzi spas, these water jet-stream gadgets can turn on your entire body. You just relax in one, sip some wine, and let the tingly bubbles soothe you all over. Warmed up and sparkling clean, you may then be in the perfect mood for more sensual explorations. We'll look at these devices in more detail in chapter 20.

17

Sensual Pleasure—
Other Senses

While touch is clearly a supreme pleasure enhancer, the other senses also offer ample opportunities for ecstasy. As with touch, the basic approach here will be to develop a connoisseur's sensibility for each sense. You want to use your imagination to find unique ways to enjoy each sense. We'll be providing practical suggestions here, but the main thing to remember is that your senses are literally the windows and doorways of your world. Once you train them to pursue a pleasure perspective, they'll afford you unlimited opportunities to appreciate life's bounties. Each year will bring a broadened enjoyment outlook, as you continually refine and sharpen your pleasure perspective.

Our culture allows more visual stimulation than perhaps any other sense. In part, this is because vision permits you to deal with things from a considerable distance—to a much greater extent than any other sense—giving you a good degree of detachment. Entire industries have been devoted to visual stimulation, and new refinements seem to be popping up all the time. TV, cinema, video games, computers and all sorts of live entertainment are just some of the choices you can now make. Vision is the key sense involved in the modern "home entertainment revolution." Pleasure philosophers are usually intrigued with high-tech home entertainment items like projector TVs, video recorders, videocassettes, home movie equipment and slide projectors. These allow visual expression on a grand scale, while giving tremendous leeway for individual tastes. You can literally orchestrate an entire evening's entertainment with such equipment.

Visual media like art and photography allow you to record and capture the world around you for the future. Bliss-seekers are always entranced by natural and man-made beauty, and the graphic arts let you share such wonders with others. Live entertainment also intensely affects the visual sense. Sporting events, performances, exhibitions, parades and the like are excellent forms of visual stimulation. Travel is another delightful pleasure for the eyes. Visiting historical sites, strange lands and unique cultures all provide engrossing visual involvement. Vacations and trips also let you dwell upon the scenic splendors of nature. Of course, the pleasure pursuer learns to exult in beauty in his immediate surroundings, as well as on long journeys. He enjoys watching attractive people, seeing sensual figures, viewing elegant clothing, or gazing at imposing architecture. The dedicated bliss-seeker will always enjoy entertainment as simple as sitting in the park and watching the birds and squirrels frolic.

Hearing, like sight, lets you maintain distance from the object you're perceiving. This is lucky indeed, because many of the sounds we're subjected to are anything but enjoyable. Most of our work life is filled with grating noises, from the

THE PLEASURE BOOK

jarring sounds of commuting to the clacking of typewriters in the office. Luckily, modern technology has come to the rescue. Most cars are now equipped with radios to mask the sounds of the road. Many people add FM stereo and cassette players to their car radios, allowing a more refined sound reception. Personal stereo cassette players like the "Walkman" became instant successes. These players, like car cassette machines, also let you listen to instructional, motivational and inspirational tapes—good, practical ways to expand your horizons. Some manufacturers even reproduce popular books on cassettes so you can use travel time to catch up on the latest literature!

If your work situation allows it, it pays to listen to the radio or music while doing your job. Light, nondistracting music works best. This won't interfere with concentration, but does provide a pleasant, uplifting background. You may not even be aware of the sound, but it will subtly enhance your mood and may even boost work performance. If your employer won't consider group-access listening, he may allow you to use a personal cassette player/radio with private headphones. But whatever auditory amusement you can obtain during work and travel time, your main pleasure will come during leisure hours. Bliss-seekers usually take great care in putting together a pleasant sound system at home, one that will allow them to enjoy stereo music and radio at its best.

Music appreciation is one of the finest forms of sound enhancement, and one can spend a lifetime developing one's tastes in this area. There are so many musical modes to choose from that it helps to keep an open mind and sample widely from classical, country, rock, jazz and blues, among other options. Different music suits different moods. Live concerts also engross you in different ways than recorded music. Some people enjoy making their own music through singing, playing an instrument, writing songs or poetry. Dancing is another unique way of responding to absorbing sound.

Nature provides many wonderful symphonies of her own. Rambling rivers, crashing waves, soft sea breezes, chirping birds, rolling thunder and gentle raindrops are some of the enchanting sounds from nature's chorus. She has also given us the varied beauty of the human voice. Apart from singing and eloquent speech, the voice also provides gutsy expression like the guttural moans and cries of lovemaking. A couple can create a melodious orchestra of its own when sharing sensual pleasures.

The sense of taste also offers ample opportunities for individual expression. Perhaps more than any other sense, taste reflects one's own uniqueness. What's junk food for one person might be gourmet dining for another. The best way to develop a refined sense of taste is to experiment and sample widely from life's broad table. Try the ethnic foods and drinks of varied cultures. Combine different items in creative ways. Some people learn about food by preparing it. Countless books and courses are available on all aspects of cooking, including Oriental cooking (wok, stir-frying), vegetarian cuisine, tofu preparations and every other ethnic style imaginable.

Some spend a lifetime developing gourmet tastes in fine food and drink. Others delight in venturing to classy restaurants. Many people make the pleasures of the palate a central part of their health program, by scientifically studying nutrition and diet. Others express their creative energies by raising their own food through gardening and sprouting. There's something particularly delectable about the taste of homegrown food. The tongue certainly provides us with one of the most intense experiences of pleasure available. It's highly sensitive to all types of textures and flavors, assuring you of multifaceted satisfactions. Chewing and swallowing also give a unique internal stimulation, as the food and drink gently stroke your innards.

THE PLEASURE BOOK

But taste pleasures are by no means limited to food. There's also the stimulating taste of the human form. The mouth and tongue are among the most tactile parts of the body. Lovers exult in intimate kissing and all its nuances: lip to lip, tongue to lips, tongue to tongue, teeth to tongue, etc. The various contours of the human frame also allow ample gustatory expression. Kisses and nibbles can be enchantingly employed on delicate areas like the neck, nipples, genitals and thighs. The pleasant taste of soft skin rates with the best culinary delights.

Our last sense, smell, is probably the most neglected of all. We have an odd ambivalence about smell which causes more disgust in us than perhaps any other sense. Freud speculated that civilization took a great leap forward when man attained an erect posture, since his nose was no longer near the ground. Unlike the other animals, man was no longer forced constantly to smell the products of his own body. Perhaps an inbred revolt against our primitive animal ancestry explains why certain smells provoke such intense responses. But annoying odors can usually be avoided easily enough. We should not allow them to make us neglect the finer aspects of our sense of smell.

The most frequent nasal enjoyment is usually associated with food. The pleasant odors of food cooking are certainly an age-old treat. Smell is an inseparable aspect of our taste sensations, as anyone with a stuffed-up nose can attest to. When your sense of smell isn't working, neither is your taste. Another ample source of olfactory enjoyment comes from nature. She provides us with a plethora of pleasant odors. People have always loved the fragrances of flowers, the salty smell of the sea, the piney odor of the forest, the clean scent of plants, the fresh smell of soil. Some animals, like cats, have a sweet natural scent on their fur, a highly pleasant experience for your nose to nestle against.

Incense and toiletries are uniquely designed for nasal delight. Incense can be used to cast a sweet fragrance throughout any room, which lends a nice romantic mood. Fragrant soaps can freshen up your bathroom. They can also provide pleasant visual stimulation, hanging on ropes or cut in unique, quaint shapes and pretty colors. Scented candles can serve similar functions in other rooms. Personal toiletries permit the ultimate in sensual olfactory expression. Perfume, cologne, musk oil, powder and body rubs exude exotic fragrances which can be highly arousing to others.

Toiletry selections can be suited to your mood and personality. The work day might call for no more than a light, pleasant scent, while lovemaking at night could require a headier, seductive aroma. Experiment to learn what suits you best at different times. The mouth can be freshened up with mouthwash, breath mints, gum or breath sprays. The nose has a unique connection with the primitive pleasure centers of the brain, making it an ideal sensual tool. The olfactory nerves link with the limbic brain, the primitive emotional center which receives maximum stimulation from the body's natural opiates, the endorphins. The nose is also one of the most sensitive tactile tissues in the body, containing the same type of erectile skin found in the genitals and erogenous zones. When the genitals are stimulated, the nose also becomes flushed with blood in a sympathetic reaction. Try burying your nose in your lover's hair or smooth skin and you may experience an associated twinge down below! At a minimum, nasal stroking produces a soothing, calming response, possibly because it may trigger endorphin release in the brain.

While perfumes and other personal toiletries can provide torrid sensual treats, a softer olfactory sensation comes from the natural scent of clean skin. Some lovers prefer the unadulterated smell of freshly showered skin to any artificial additives. Rub your nose lightly over your lover's skin, both sniffing and touching, and enjoy the pleasant stimulation. Other people are turned on by the natural odors of the

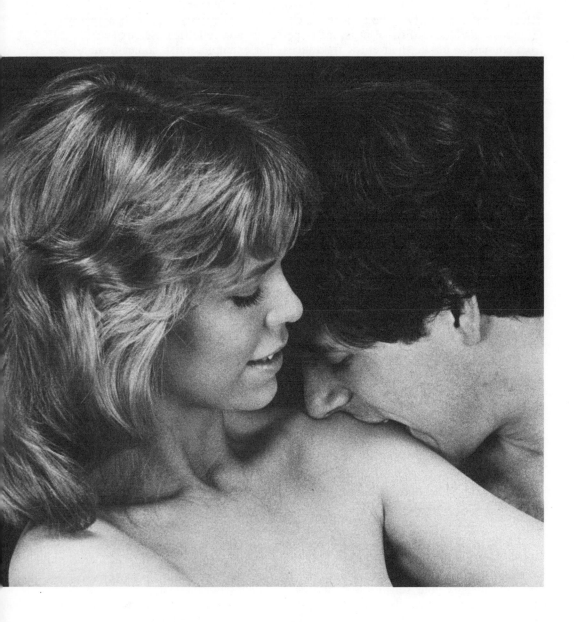

body. Some lovers delight in the smell and taste of their partner's sexual secretions. Some are even turned on by the smell of their lover's sweat! There's actually nothing "dirty" about such smells; our squeamish culture has just drummed this idea into us. Fact is, many perfumes and toiletries use sex scents from animals to create their erotic fragrances. For example, musk comes from a sac beneath the abdominal skin of the male musk deer. If other species can stimulate us so much, it stands to reason that human sex scents should be equally effective, if not more potent. Let go of the dictates of our hygiene-obsessed society and really check out your lover's body. You may discover a whole new world of sensual and olfactory sweetness just waiting for you!

One of the most pleasurable ways to employ your senses is by creatively combining them. As we indicated in an earlier chapter, certain senses blend particularly well. Taste and smell are natural partners, as are hearing and sight. Visual and tactile stimulation merge quite nicely, as any artist knows. One of the most versatile combinations is sight, sound and touch. Modern high-tech advances seem to recognize this. The home entertainment center seems to be leading the field. Comfortably enfolded in cushy, futuristic furniture like bean bags and air-inflated pillows, the home entertainment buff's tactile senses are nicely soothed.

Without having to move an inch, he can use a remote-control device to switch on his giant projector TV and enjoy topflight visual excitement from cable, pay TV, satellite reception, videocassettes and laser disks. The pictures may even come in 3-D holographic effect. And of course, the entire setup will be hooked into the finest available sound system, filling the entire room with pulsating vibrations. He'll likely be surrounded by multiple speaker channels which will make a live orchestra seem dull by comparison. And this is just the mainstream of what's being offered in home entertainment. At the leading edge, robots are now being manufactured which will not only bring you your favorite drinks or snacks, but vacuum the house as well. You can also overwhelm your senses with multimedia projectors, laser-beam light shows, holographic 3-D images, black lights, strobes, multicolored flashing crystal ceiling lights and who knows what else.

The ecstasy explosion is hardly limited to the living room. The bathroom is fast becoming a sensorium. Shower-massagers titillate our tactile nerves, and portable saunas refresh our pores. Hot tubs and Jacuzzi spas afford optimum sensory enhancement. The time is ripe for a merger of the electronic revolution and hydromassage inventions. One can easily envision a Jacuzzi- or hot tub–filled room decked out with lavish quadrophonic sound equipment and video gadgetry. A flip of a switch will tune you into your giant projector TV, or perhaps you'd prefer *a pulsating light show as you soak in your bubbly jet-stream tub.* And of course, Fred the Robot will be there to get whatever you want in the way of food and drink. Fantasyland? Hardly—it's right around the corner.

Whether or not you choose the high-tech route to external sensory enjoyment, you can intensify your sensory experiences markedly from the inside. There are chemical substances available to alter sense perceptions in nearly any way you want. But remember, many are illegal and/or unhealthy. We'll examine them in more detail in a later chapter, but a brief mention is warranted here. Naturally, any discussion of drugs must start with America's most popular, alcohol. In moderate amounts, alcohol can be pleasant and stimulating, but too much will put you "out of it" in no time. For relaxation, there's no shortage of tranquilizers available: hypnotics, soporifics, barbiturates, etc. Stronger effects can be attained from the opiate group, including morphine and codeine. But, tranquilizers and opiates really take you away from your senses rather than enhance them.

As for sensory enhancers, marijuana and its derivatives stimulate all your sense receptors from taste to touch. Some people swear it heightens their lovemaking, but the chemical with the real reputation in that category is amyl nitrite and its variants ("poppers"). By increasing the heart rate, pulse, respiration and generally exciting the body, poppers mimic the phases of sexual excitement. Its adherents claim it intensifies the erotic experience markedly. Others feel it scares them and gives them a headache.

Another reputed "love drug" is the nonhallucinogenic psychedelic, MDA. It was out of circulation for some time, but underground labs are churning it out again, with the greatest demand from the gay community. It's supposed to enhance sensuality, possibly by slowing down the sexual reactions. Some swear by it, others consider it a dud.

No discussion about drugs would be complete without mentioning the stimulants: cocaine, amphetamines, speed, etc. They can enliven things for a while, but their tension-causing, stressful effects make them less-than-ideal sense boosters. If you really want to enjoy a sensual smorgasbord, artificial aids are unnecessary and can be harmful. A nice bout of intense lovemaking with a favorite pleasure-partner is all you really need.

18
Sexual Attitudes

No one will deny that sexual bliss is at the top of any pleasure hierarchy. Unfortunately, it's also historically been a key target for many of the heaviest pleasure prohibitions. Earlier, we looked at some of the ways cultures stifled full expression of the sex drive. Mercifully, we have advanced eons beyond the old sexual attitudes which considered anything connected with the body sinful and dirty. In all but the most prudish and narrow-minded circles, sexual fulfillment is considered normal and natural. The sexual revolution has introduced the idea of sexual expression as an inalienable right. People without regular sex lives nowadays are considered deprived and unbalanced.

The most drastic shift in attitudes has been in the area of female sexual roles. The outmoded Victorian model had women as passive vehicles for male sexual expression. "Lie back and endure" was the prevailing view, which persisted pretty much through the mid-twentieth century. Female sexual enjoyment was once heresy; the rare woman who admitted pleasure publicly would be considered lecherous or whorish. Her orgasmic ability was almost unknown; her role was limited to a tool for male sex gratification. Sex was simply a brutish, animal force which swept over the male, overwhelming his better nature and making him defile the female. The shorter the act, the better. Not surprisingly, this was the era of the all-purpose "headache," a woman's excuse to avoid sex whenever possible. And with these attitudes, it's not hard to see why.

These antiquated ideas eroded with Freud's revelations about sex, then were turned upside down by the sexual revolution. While there's still plenty of prudery, it's far from fashionable or sophisticated. The sexual revolution, aided by modern birth control, encouraged all sorts of sexual experimentation. But it took the women's liberation movement to bring female sex instincts fully out of the closet. As feminists have pointed out, the sexual revolution was mostly a license for male sexual explorations of women. During the "free love" period of the sixties, men often had the luxury of several accommodating sex partners. Women who were reluctant were often pressured with accusations of being "uptight" or "frigid." There was plenty of sex, but women were still, by and large, silent partners. A radical shift came about when feminism, armed with late-breaking research about female sexual potency, insisted that women deserved fulfillment too.

As research revealed the power of female sex drives and desires, the "right to orgasm" became a hot topic. Women actively revolted against the old "wham bam, thank you ma'am" sexual pattern in which intercourse was completed in a few minutes. Men were pressured to hold back ejaculation until their partners were also sated. Studies then showed that women were multiorgasmic, capable of coming time and time again during the same sex act. More research showed that all female orgasms were centered in the clitoris, making it crucial for men to learn to stimulate this small spot directly.

So the sexually liberated woman now expected her lovers to be impeccable sexual technicians. They should be able to hold an erection as long as needed, and be very capable in the arts of oral and manual stimulation. Moreover, they should be experts in the art of foreplay, since it was now known that female arousal was a slow, gradual process. They also should be excellent in afterplay, since you never could tell when more than one female orgasm was in the making. And they should be knowledgeable about all sexual positions, because women now knew that the "missionary posture," with the man on top, was not optimal for clitoral stimulation. Finally, they should be able to orchestrate the entire affair. Women's liberation obviously turned the old Victorian ideas upside down and inside out. But ironically, it replaced one set of negative attitudes with another equally destructive set.

Presently, sex therapists' offices are flooded with men reporting severe impotency problems. Men are intimidated by the new female expectations, especially the implied demand to bring their partners to orgasm all the time. The multiple-orgasm capacity of women has created even more confusion and bewilderment for men. Some have been badgered and humiliated by partners for not "keeping it up" long enough; others for not stimulating their lover's clitoris "the right way," orally or manually; and others for not being able to maintain different sexual positions.

"I don't know what to do to please her," is a common complaint therapists hear. "She never gives me any hints or feedback, but expects me to know exactly what to do and when to do it." Many of these problems stem from a single issue, an area that the feminist critique pretty much overlooked. That is, the outmoded role of the male as the controller of the sex act.

The feminists pounded away long and hard on the female right to sexual pleasure, but they placed most of the responsibility for this pleasure squarely on male shoulders. Ironically, this is little more than a sophisticated version of the Victorian view of the female as passive recipient—only this time, the male was not only expected to gratify himself, but her as well! Although there are some enlightened feminists who now believe that a woman's sexual fulfillment is "her own responsibility," the average woman still expects her mate to bear a disproportionate burden. Popular sex manuals, with countless depictions of acrobatic-style sex postures only superhumans could pull off, have hardly helped. In fact, the all-time best-selling handbook *The Joy of Sex* was classified by one of the major wire services as fiction!

For many men, the result has been all sorts of sexual dysfunctions with foreboding clinical names like "premature ejaculation," "performance anxiety" and "castration complex." To add to the intimidation, new sexual goals continued to be uncovered on a regular basis. The latest is the so-called G-spot, purportedly a glandlike tissue on the upper inside wall of the vagina. Stimulation of this spot supposedly leads to "cosmic orgasms" accompanied by "gushing ejaculations." Although subsequent studies indicate that large percentages of women derive no pleasure there, and the touted ejaculation appears to be ordinary urine, these revelations did not prevent some from publicizing detailed instructions to show men how to reach this new sexual goal. Needless to say, many men who jumped on the G-spot bandwagon found nothing but further reason to feel inadequate.

Sex therapists, the professionals who hear the most sex problems, often exacerbate the difficulties by buying right into antiquated myths about male sexual performance. For instance, countless numbers of therapy hours are spent dealing with the big bugaboo, "premature ejaculation." But has anyone ever considered the idea of women having "premature orgasms"? The notion sounds absurd, but

only because of the prevailing bias against men. Some women can indeed come shortly after introduction of the penis, while the male is still thrusting, but most would view such a female not as inadequate, but as exceedingly erotic. A similar example is the idea of "performance anxiety." This too is almost solely limited to men; they are the ones who worry about climaxing too soon, or being clumsy, inept or unskilled. Women are rarely judged as sexual performers. In fact, the sign of a "good" female lover often rests upon what she *doesn't do*—on how passive, yielding, receptive and cooperative she is.

The fact is, a pernicious, pervasive double standard exists for sexuality, a standard that's reinforced by most sex therapies. The female is required to do little more than just relax and play along, while the male is expected to be the well-primed sex machine. He's supposed to be the knowledgeable, skilled sex technician, the well-trained mechanism finely tuned to perform on command. It's expected that his erections will appear at will, and he will be unaffected by anxiety, fear and insecurity. When two lovers connect for the first time, the man is usually quite concerned with how she'll compare him to her other partners, while he hardly ever cares about how she'll stack up against his former flames. The old Victorian idea of the male as the sole sexual "doer" is very much alive, though subtly hidden in the sophisticated rhetoric of the sexual revolution.

Sex therapists make large sums of money treating performance-related problems like premature ejaculation, problems which are part and parcel of the sexual double standard. Actually, if these antiquated ideas were finally put to rest, many so-called sex problems would disappear as well. On a purely human level, the idea of delaying one's sexual release is totally unnatural and antibiological. Since no one ever expects women to postpone climaxes, why are men routinely expected to? The sole rationale is that the male's partner may not be satisfied if he comes first. But that's another key fallacy: female needs can be satisfied many ways, and intercourse is not always the most effective one. If a man should come before his lover, there are plenty of other things that can be done. He can stimulate her orally or manually, or use a vibrator, or he can also just cuddle with her until his erection returns.

THE PLEASURE BOOK

There are also many other so-called performance problems which dissolve when one employs a more humane viewpoint—for example, the grand quest for "simultaneous orgasm," in which both lovers come at the same moment. This leads to an even worse unnatural delay than the premature ejaculation myth! Women like the idea of having control over their bodies, and men should take exactly the same view—which means *no person, sex therapist or sex manual should allow a man to feel guilty about the length of time it takes him to climax.* This is purely his right and prerogative. If men accept this idea and respect their own natural rhythms, there will be much less concern over "performance." A truly free sexual ethic would eradicate this subtle double standard and view male and female as fully equal partners in sexual pleasure. Men would no longer be take-charge, all-doer sex props and women would no longer be passive, do-nothing sex objects.

An enlightened sexual attitude is one where all types of sex play are okay as long as no one is harmed. This opens up all sorts of erotic explorations, including oral, manual and anal play. No judgments, put-downs or preconceived expectations, just two people being together to share sexual bliss. Everyone would recognize that both male and female are subject to fear, vulnerability and anxiety. Men could relax and express their passive side, while women could be uninhibited about showing their active side.

Sex could become transformed from a win-lose game to a shared pleasure pursuit. Without the heavy load of cultural and "therapeutic" stereotypes, lovers could express a childlike, innocent curiosity about each other's body. The body would become a fertile playground for all types of exciting explorations. By loosening rigid social restrictions and "proper" and "improper" sexuality, repressed erotic energy would be released, leading in many cases to increased potency.

Rid yourself of deep-rooted inhibitions and inflexible ideas about male and female functions. As an alternative, try an open-minded, "anything-goes," "hang-loose" approach. Forget about performance and the 57 varieties of the sex manuals. Don't judge your partners and don't allow yourself to be judged either. Try this and you may find new, unimagined power springing up in your sex life.

Beneath all this cultural conditioning may well be a childlike, spontaneous approach to sex. Freud described infants as "polymorphous perverse," meaning that their bodies were one unified erogenous zone, and that they could literally get into any type of erotic play if not tamed by civilization. From Freud's view, the "polymorphous" phase was an infantile state which was gradually transcended as one grew, until the genitals became the main focus of sexual feeling. But, Freud's view was only partially true.

It's more likely that Freud's "sexual maturation" stage reflected the prudish ideas of his Victorian milieu more than any biological realities. We seem now to be rediscovering the full erotic potential of our body, that in fact it is capable of sensual and sexual pleasure in all areas. This is clearly reflected in the overwhelming popularity of full-body experiences like massage, shiatsu, hot tubs, etc. The purely genital focus on sex, dominant for so long, is rapidly being replaced by interest in stimulation of the body as a whole.

My view is that adults retain their inborn polymorphous sensitivities, even though much of our moral propaganda puts a lid on its expression. For example, in almost all states the only legal way to make love is through "missionary posture" intercourse (man on top) between married couples. Any other activities could land you in jail, although almost everyone, including legal officials, all but ignores these outmoded statutes.

But it does seem that we are in the midst of a renaissance of the body. The

reemergence of polymorphous sexuality in adult life fits this trend quite nicely. I think a great model of unbiased, natural sexuality can be seen in the way young children act. They treat each other's bodies as objects of mystery and wonder, and invent cute little games which allow them to explore every nook and cranny. The classic game is "doctor," in which kids take turns examining each other via the roles of patient and physician. It's fascinating how intrigued they are with their biology, how they want to compare organs, probe orifices, etc.

They rarely give a hoot about which sex they're playing with, as they haven't been preconditioned with homophobia. They display a wonderful, innocent, natural spontaneity and curiosity. And most intriguing, these young children are not yet even capable of sex. They can neither copulate nor achieve orgasm, and yet they still display intense interest in their bodies and their function. Unfortunately, in most cases this innocence is punished as soon as adults learn about their play. Obviously, childhood explorations are extremely threatening to the rigid preconceptions of conventional morality.

Despite this negative cultural conditioning, I think the ideal situation between lovers would be to recapture the attitude of polymorphous perversity. Then you could drop all the macho roles and female facades. You would just have two people doing whatever felt right in a natural, innocent, guiltless way. Christ once remarked that "ye must be as little children to enter the kingdom of God." What he meant was childlike wonder and innocence were preconditions for entering paradise. He also said that the "kingdom of God is within you." Put these statements together and it's hard to escape the conclusion that the return to childlike, unjaded attitudes is the key to fulfilling your inner potential. At the least, the childlike attitude is an ideal way to maximize your sexual pleasure possibilities.

19

Sexual Pleasure

Sexual joy can be truly appreciated only when you've rid yourself of most of the antierotic attitudes discussed in the last chapter. Your mind will then be free of restrictive ideas about eroticism. Once that's accomplished, you'll be liberated from the twin prisons of prudery and performance anxiety. You'll be open and receptive to all forms of sexual novelty, not controlled by rigid ideas about sex roles and taboos. You won't be quick to condemn your partner's sexual creativity. Like someone sampling a new ethnic food, you won't pass judgment until you've savored it.

The first rule of sexual pleasure involves an inviting setting. Some of the most satisfying escapades occur outside the home. Vacationers relish fond memories of exciting encounters on exotic beaches, secluded, sun-drenched paradises, or remote sea cruises. Even if you can't afford such extravagant adventures, there may be exceedingly romantic opportunities close by. For example, places like the Pocono mountains in Pennsylvania offer "lovers' retreats" replete with oversize heart-shaped tubs, Jacuzzis, private swimming pools, beautiful scenic views and other amenities to fire up your intimate appetites. If a weekend at a pleasure palace like this doesn't suit your fancy, a trip to a local motel may fit the bill. Many motels, usually located on the outskirts of town, offer water beds and large-screen color TVs featuring adult movies. Such escapes take you out of your normal routine and spice up what may have become a dull, uncreative sex life.

All couples should regularly schedule a "pleasure vacation." It can be as exotic as an ocean cruise or as simple as a short motel stop, but the notion is the same. You want to get away from your home base to explore new environments and events. Ideally, the new setting should offer wonderful romantic diversions like elegant architecture, beautiful surroundings, fine entertainment, delightful cuisine, recreation facilities and the like. But as nice as these amenities can be, the real object is personal privacy, getting far away from the daily grind. Some couples on pleasure vacations actually ignore the local attractions and hang the "do not disturb" sign on the door during their entire stay. This is by no means a bad idea, since the main reason for a pleasure vacation is to focus your attention on each other, not on the outside world.

Fortunately, the creative couple need not be on vacation to enjoy unique sexual experiments. A romantic setting can also be created at home. You need little more than a clean, comfortable abode, soft lighting, candles, incense and some nice music. The only absolute requirement is an open mind and willingness to explore. A nice warm-up for many lovers can be adult video programming, either from cable systems with X-rated movies, or from X-rated video disks or cassettes. Some lovers film their own erotic episodes and play them on their video recorders. Other warm-up possibilities are various "strip games" in which garments are removed one at a time. There are many such games available on the market, or you can devise your own with cards or by "spinning the bottle." An even more risqué version is to have the "winner" tell the "loser" what sexual fantasy he'd like the latter to perform as a "penalty" for losing. Games like these generate excitement in anticipation of what is to come.

There are numerous ways to make any phase of an erotic involvement into a titillating, thrilling affair. We've already mentioned several sensual methods which can comfortably precede sex: shiatsu, massage and cuddling. All of these techniques will relax, stimulate and warm you up for greater intimacy. The act of disrobing can be an erotic art form in itself. Some lovers enjoy lying back and watching a "striptease" act in which their partners slowly, tantalizingly take off one item at a time, proceeding from the most innocent to the most intimate garment. Others thrill at the idea of being disrobed by their partners bit by bit in a slow, sensual fashion. Once his lover is fully naked, the active partner should take some time to gaze at his lover's form, imagining the supreme pleasures it will soon afford him.

A disrobing ritual can also include a practice called "body worship." The naked partner stands there while the active lover circles around, hungrily contemplating the treasures he's about to enjoy. The standing partner grows tingly in anticipation. The active partner eventually zeroes in on a body spot of his lover, covering it with gentle nibbles and kisses. He may pick an innocent area like the feet or an erotic zone like the thighs, or an out-and-out erogenous area like the buttocks, genitals or nipples. He may then move his partner into new positions, such as bending over, to afford even greater access to the spot he's picked. Eventually, he'll lead his lover to the bed, where he may continue his attentions, or start some new erotic stimulation.

Naturally, every modern adult is familiar with the basic forms of love play, but ordinary erotic activities can always be enhanced with variety and experimentation. This may mean looking into rarely used sexual postures. Check out your prevailing sex positions. Do you pretty much stick to a standard routine of kissing, foreplay and intercourse? Try to alter this predictable routine. How about a full-body mouth massage, covering your partner with sweet wet caresses from head to toe? Or much more extensive foreplay, touching your friend all over, not only on the genitals. Or extended oral-genital stimulation, maybe even to orgasm. Too many lovers cheat themselves and their partners by not exploring the supreme exaltation of orally induced release.

Anal eroticism is a neglected sexual variation. The entire anal area is surrounded by sensitive nerve endings, much more so than the interior of the vaginal canal. Both men and women report highly stimulating sensations inside the anus and around the skin between the genitals and anus. Pressing the latter spot on men has been known to arouse them, but can also be used to delay orgasm during sex,

137

THE PLEASURE BOOK   .

thus prolonging the act. Anal intercourse has always been popular with men, since the female rectal opening offers tightness on the male shaft. Some precautions are in order, however: sufficient lubrication is needed (a water-soluble gel like KY is best). You must also avoid going from anal to regular intercourse, since rectal bacteria can be harmful to the vagina. And of course, you must be sensitive, tender and nonforceful during the act itself.

Men can also enjoy anal penetration. Interviews with prostitutes reveal that a common male fantasy is to be penetrated by a dildo-bearing dominant female. But short of that, you can also probe with a thin, specially shaped anal vibrator attachment or fingers (closely cropped nails, naturally). Lubricant is useful here as well. The prostate gland (the male "P-spot") is highly sensitive and can be reached by rubbing a finger against the upper rectal wall, toward the base of the penis shaft. Some men actually report orgasm from P-spot stimulation alone. Just make sure you're gentle and careful when probing this area. The real problem with anal play for both sexes is the deeply engrained taboo against anything associated with human waste material.

Fortunately, there is a remedy, one which can produce lots of pleasure in itself. A couple bent on anal delights can make cleansing rituals an aspect of sex play. They can bathe and shower each other, paying particular attention to the nether parts.

Game playing can be used to enhance your sex life. Role switching can be a real turn-on, with the male playing passive and the female aggressive. Sexual role-playing can also include full-fledged costumes. A trip to a costume rental shop can produce garb for popular games like Princess/Knight, Countess/Beggar, Troubador/Maiden, Caveman/Cavegirl, King/Queen, Magician/Helper, etc. You can work out a seduction script beforehand, or just spontaneously wing it. Paraphernalia can include flowers, a grail, magical elixir (champagne, sparkling cider, etc.), musical instruments and incense. You can set up a courtship ceremony which will inevitably lead to magical lovemaking. Such rituals tap the creative powers of the mind, introducing fantasy, imagination and aggressive instincts into your sex play. The games also introduce an important element of "otherness" between you, since the roles make you strangers of sorts, even if only in play. This "stranger" element adds new zest to what can become routine involvement for regular sex partners.

Another novel sex technique worth mentioning is a modern variation of ancient Eastern erotic traditions like Tantric yoga. In these systems, sex was used as a mystical force, a means of raising potent spiritual energies between the participating couple. The idea was to delay male ejaculation indefinitely so the energies grew unbelievably powerful. Sex positions which prevented quick ejaculation were employed, the most common being the female on top. After penetration, the couple either moved slowly or just stood still, not trying to thrust hard for fulfillment. If male ejaculation seemed imminent, movements ceased totally until the urge passed. Then they were resumed, with the energy level being raised each time.

A full Tantric-type session could last for hours, with the couple eventually feeling totally spaced out by sexual energies. Eventually, a totally mystical state was achieved, called "samsara," "nirvana" or "cosmic consciousness." Your lover came to be seen as a Godlike figure. Modern versions of these arts claim that men can achieve orgasm this way—in fact many times—without ejaculation (female orgasms were always considered okay). However, many of these systems were based on the ancient idea that male ejaculation robbed him of vital life energy and fluids. Holding back ejaculation indefinitely is a steeper price than most of us care to pay, even for "cosmic consciousness." A better idea is to try some of these techniques, build up the potent energy for some time, then finally release the full flood of stored-up seminal fluid. With the male staying erect so long, the female is not likely to be left wanting. You'll both have had a fine taste of transcendent experience, topped off by a frenzied, ecstatic orgasm.

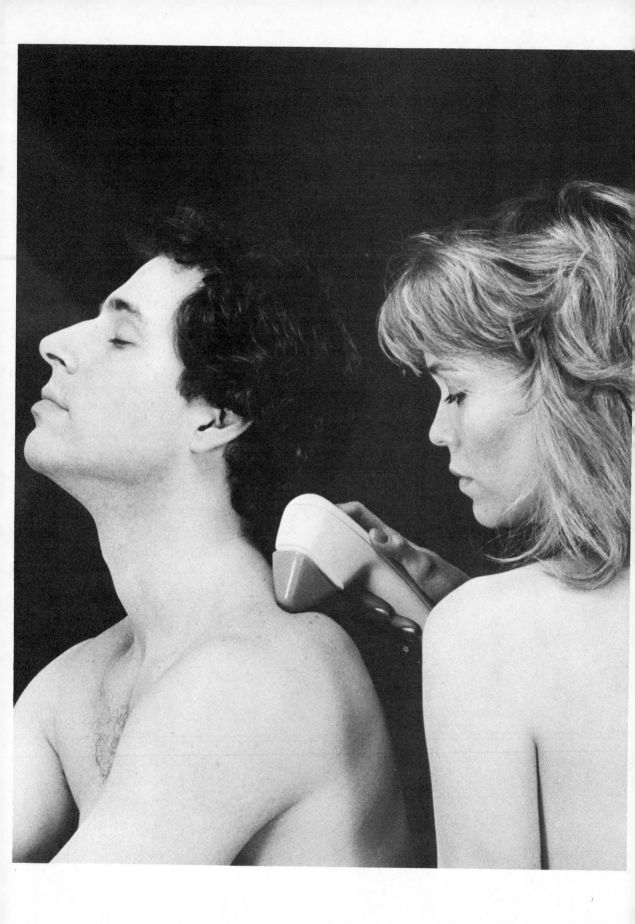

20

Pleasure Products

The world abounds in natural pleasures, including beautiful beaches, wonderful wildernesses, majestic mountains, and luxurious lakes. The body itself is a bountiful source, with the senses and sexual instincts all adding varied enjoyments. Love, friendship, caring and sharing are among the social pleasures we can all exult in. But nature has by no means exhausted the pleasure quest, for technological innovations throughout history have greatly aided the process. Most of man's inventions have been designed to lessen drudgery and labor. Seminal advancements like the wheel, engine, telephone, steamboat and electricity have immeasurably lightened life's chores. People have not only been freed from painful, beastly burdens, but they've been given increased leisure time to do what they want.

Labor-saving devices are always appreciated, and it's hoped that the future will bring more ways to travel, shop, communicate, bank, clean and carry out other needed tasks. But we're more interested here in items which clearly pack a pleasure payoff of their own, apart from the time or labor saved. As our culture slowly emerges from the weakening constraints of the pleasure prohibitions, pleasure technologies seem to be cropping up all over. Pleasure angles are being exploited by products formerly associated with other functions, like hygiene. Manufacturers are jumping onto the bandwagon, with product packaging and ads pitching enjoyment. Even commercials, which usually reflect cultural values, are parlaying hedonist themes ("you only go round once in life, so you might as well grab all the gusto you can").

Some of these are good signs, but one also must remember that the basic business of business is to sell, and Madison Avenue quickly capitalizes on trends in ways that suit its interests best. You must beware of many of the pseudopleasures on the market, products which produce temporary satiation and long-term disintegration. For example, the ads for tobacco, hard liquor and fancy cars are replete with depictions of elegant people, high-society life, sexy companions, etc. They are trying to exploit your pleasure drive and seduce you into using their products. The health effects of smoking are well known, and as we noted earlier, it's a product that won't boost your pleasure capacities. Alcoholism has little more to say for it, though moderate use of softer alcoholic products presents no major problems. The thoughtful bliss-seeker is indeed a hedonist, but a *healthy hedonist,* as we pointed out before—and generally a socially conscious one as well. His creative, active lifestyle will assure him of *genuine pleasure*—the sex, popularity and success which products like these falsely promise.

Many of the pleasure technologies which are truly healthful have received scant media attention because they've been quietly manufactured by people who shun mass-market hype. One example is the "body roller," a wooden object which

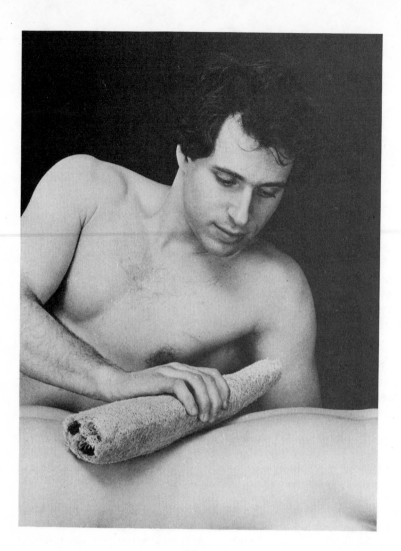

comes in various sizes. The rollers are used to stimulate acupuncture points along the spine, feet and other spots, thus allowing a sort of do-it-yourself shiatsu treatment. They are usually available in health food stores. A more well-known pleasure product is the "mechanical massager," a device available with attachments for all types of bodily stimulation. The most prevalent type is a hand-held gadget the size of a phone handle, with detachable devices for massaging the face, scalp, muscles, etc. They usually also come with a knob-shaped "spot stimulator," basically meant for clitoral strokes. The Prelude models, the most popular ones among connoisseurs of these products, can also be purchased with a special attachment designed for penis stimulation, as well as other explicitly sexual attachments. Other mechanical massager variations include the "wand," a longer unit for hard-to-reach places, and the "twin-head unit," reportedly great for penis stimulation. These gadgets can be used for a stimulating massage, and are also useful as aids to induce female orgasm (although they should not be confused with battery-operated "vibrators"). Prelude publishes a sensitive instructional booklet which shows a couple how it can be used to overcome orgasmic inhibitions.

While the mechanical massagers can be used to supplement hand massage, a better bet is the "Swedish-style" massagers which you strap to the back of your hand. These units, put out by manufacturers like Oster and Pollenex, vibrate your hand, so you touch your partner not with plastic or metal, but with your own skin. Many professional massage therapists use the Swedish units as adjuncts to standard hand massage. There are other types of massage products available, according to your taste. Some combine heat with vibrating action, others can be lain up on ("cushion massagers"), and still others help out tired feet. Oster and Clairol put out "foot massagers," small plastic tubs which let your feet soak in hot water with whirlpool action. Mechanical massagers can generally be bought in drug stores, department stores, gift shops and novelty stores like New York's Hammacher Schlemmer.

Another popular massage device is the shower massage attachment. This allows you to change a normal shower spray into a pulsating, throbbing beat of water whose tempo you can control. Shower massagers are made by various manufacturers, including Teledyne, and can easily be bought at retail outlets. They come in several varieties, including a "steamer" model which is supposed to turn your shower stall into a miniature steamroom. These products work well after rough exercise, when sore muscles really benefit from warm, pulsating water.

Other pleasure-producing products make use of water in even more creative ways. "Hydro-massage," the rapid circulation of water around the body, has been shown in medical literature to help alleviate ailments like arthritis, muscle sprains, etc. You can actually purchase a portable device which will hook to your bathtub and create a soothing whirlpool effect right there as you soak. More elaborate variations include the Jacuzzi spa, a special oversized fiberglass tub equipped with swirling water jets. These can be built to any size or shape. A more rustic version · is the California hot tub, a craze which is sweeping the nation. The hot tub is usually a freestanding, barrellike wooden fixture, attached to pumps which circulate soothing air jets around the tub. Water temperature is controlled, so you can luxuriate in an outdoor tub even on a cold wintry night. Hot tubs can be built large enough for a half dozen dunkers or more and special trays can be added to hold wine, cheese or other favorites.

Another interesting pleasure device also has profound health and hygiene effects. This is the European-style sauna, an enclosed wooden structure which is superheated by a stove. Hot stones on top of the stove are splashed with water to produce steam, which has an exhilarating effect on the lungs. A popular sauna tradition is to become thoroughly heated, then go outside and jump into an icy winter lake, river or tub. This cold plunge is one of the high points of the experience. In some climes, a dive in a snowdrift is used! Some sauna enthusiasts repeat the hot/cold cycle many times in one session. An American Indian version is called "sweats," where a dozen or so people huddle in a closed structure around a pit filled with burning hot rocks. The medicine man performs a healing ceremony, part of which consists of spurts of water being cast on the rocks, causing stimulating bursts of steam. You may feel faint at first, but if you hang in there, a thorough cleansing occurs. When you emerge into the cold open air afterwards, your body is so supercharged with heat that that seemingly unthinkable dip in icy water seems quite appropriate. I've seen "sweats" enthusiasts hanging around unclothed on winter mornings after a session, as though it were a July day on the beach.

Saunas and sweats release accumulated toxins and poisons in your body. The Indian ceremony also contributes healing energies for all types of emotional, physical and psychological ills. But even the ordinary sauna has added pluses, including improved circulation and profound relaxation. Some authorities also claim a "heightened tactile sense" which lingers for hours after the session. If this is true, you should find sensual experiences nicely enhanced. While most people enjoy serene relaxation after, sensual or sexual play works as well.

Some sauna enthusiasts go to the trouble of building their own hothouses, while others take advantage of sauna facilities in local health clubs or resorts; but some companies are making miniature steam generators to turn your private stall shower into a steam bath. You can also try certain shower massage attachments, noted above, which include steamer capacities.

A new trend among pleasure enthusiasts is the tranquility tank, the invention of Dr. John Lilly, well-known researcher in diverse areas like dolphin communication and consciousness expansion. The unit, also called an "isolation tank," contains an epsom-salt solution which allows your body to float freely on the water's surface. The film *Altered States* showed the tanks being used in a fantasy context. The epsom-salt solution removes normal muscle tension caused by the ordinary workings of gravity. The small chamber is also sight- and soundproof, allowing you to voyage into inner space. You become aware of things you never knew before, like internal body sounds, then you reach a stage of total transcendence. With the body thoroughly relaxed and quieted, your mind roams freely throughout the psychic universe. Many strange revelations get reported, as well as a total relaxation and inner peace. The units can be bought for twenty-five hundred dollars or so, but most people go to local health centers and rent an hour's use for twenty to twenty-five dollars. These tanks should enjoy increasing popularity.

Another water-intensive pleasure product is the good old water bed. People who've tried these report that they aid sleep by conforming to the body's curves. There's also something very soothing about floating freely in the wavelike ripples of the bed. This gentle movement is something like being rocked in a cradle. It also provides an enticing accompaniment for lovemaking, the real bonus in water beds. Lovers report that their movements are tenderly reinforced by the slight ripples. The undulating effects let your bodies merge and flow with the water's rhythms. Some pleasure-connoisseurs use a regular mattress for sleep, with a second water bed as part of their personal "pleasure den."

Water has other uses for pleasure than those we've just discussed. The old-fashioned, leisurely soak in the bathtub—with or without a partner—is a wonderful way to ward off the cares of the world. It loosens tense muscles, enhances circulation, reduces stress and removes gravity's strain on the bones. You can make a bath a royal occasion with bubble products, bath oils, fragrant soaps, bath mits, loofahs and inflatable plastic bath pillows. You can add to the atmosphere by dimming the lights, putting on pleasant music and sipping a favorite drink. If you bathe with a buddy, you can both wash, towel, oil, powder and caress each other. Alone or accompanied, the bath can be a regular retreat from the daily grind.

Skin-care products offer another avenue for creative pleasure. Technology has now come up with devices with cleaning attachments for the face and other areas. Some of these brushlike attachments feel quite nice stroking the skin while they remove dead tissue or apply creams. Many people enjoy the pampering of beauty salons, where you can luxuriate in a manicure or facial masque with sweet-smelling herbs. If you really want to go full tilt, visit a fully equipped health spa or retreat, where you can enjoy all types of pleasure aids, like saunas, pools, Jacuzzis, gourmet foods, recreation and sometimes natural hot springs. Check each resort for a full list of amenities.

There are also all sorts of aids available to enhance sexual bliss. These range anywhere from battery-operated vibrators to "french ticklers" for clitoral stimulation to "pneumatic tubes" for mechanical masturbation. There are creams and lotions to enhance oral play, and gadgets of all shapes to insert in all sorts of

intimate spots. Some cities feature elegant sex boutiques like New York's Eve's Garden, where you can browse around for such items; catalogues can also be ordered from the back pages of men's erotic magazines. Less savory settings for shopping for such products are the "adult book shop/peep show" establishments.

Technological innovation has also provided a plethora of more refined pleasure products. For example, research has shown that "positive ions"—charges in the air produced by environmental conditions like rain—contribute to sour moods. Negative ions, usually associated with clear, sunny days, produce more cheerful states of mind. You can purchase "negative ion generators" which will lift your mood. You can also buy "fresh air machines"; "white sound generators" to help you sleep; "relaxation bars" which let you hang upside down, bringing blood to your head; neck rests to reduce tension there; down comforters to keep you cozy and warm; "shiatsu sandals" to stimulate your soles; "skip joggers" for stationary exercise; and beds you can adjust so you can sit up and read.

Other technological wizardry includes cordless phones, portable gyms, miniature TVs, projector TVs, every computer aid imaginable, portable biofeedback monitors and even miniature robots. If multimedia light shows turn you on, you can pick up the Edmund Scientific Catalog (Barrington, New Jersey) and purchase hologram devices which project 3-D images in the room, or a complete portable light show featuring kaleidoscopic projectors, psychedelic wheels, strobe lights, etc. Other sources for pleasure technology include the *Sharper Image Catalog* (San Francisco) and *Whole Life Times* (found in health food stores). If you happen to be looking for a gift for "someone who has everything," try some of these products!

21

Other Pleasure Pursuits

Pleasure is as broad as the entire spectrum of human experience, so there's no way to fully capture it inside the covers of a small book. We've provided extensive insights and suggestions, paying particular attention to pleasure subjects which warrant full treatment. But there are many odds and ends we haven't thoroughly examined. One of the most significant is the area of drugs, recreational chemicals people use to alter consciousness. Throughout history, men have sought new substances to shift mood, eliminate pain, and change sensory awareness. Some observers speculate that this ancient quest reveals an innate pleasure drive. Whether or not that's so, it's an undeniable fact that people do use drugs, legal or otherwise, to change consciousness, and no amount of sermonizing or law enforcement has ever done much to dissuade them. Therefore, it's useful to present an objective, unbiased account of how drugs affect pleasure.

Most people think that drugs are ideal pleasure tools, but many drugs are really pseudopleasures which dull your senses. For example, chemicals like the opiates (narcotics), barbiturates, quaaludes ("downers") and the like may make you feel a pleasant, hazy euphoria, but this is really a dulling of true pleasure sensation. Light doses of minor tranquilizers like Valium can serve to relax you and release inhibitions, but in larger doses they merely blot out sense perceptions. The same goes for heavier tranquilizers like thorazine, stelazine and haldol. These psychiatric drugs can render you a walking zombie, hardly a state of bliss.

Another popular, but very dangerous group, are the stimulants. These include diet pills, amphetamines and cocaine. These substances produce a temporary euphoric sensation which is usually followed by deep depression as the drugs wear off. They also interfere with blood flow and appetite and have many deleterious side effects. They can hardly be considered pleasure enhancers. The same goes for the substance Madison Avenue spends millions pushing as a pleasure avenue: cigarettes. Smoking cuts your breathing—your basic life energies—and makes you less sensitive to sensory excitement. People interpret the transient calmness and feelings of "fullness" caused by smoking to be enjoyable. Actually, long-term results include excessive wrinkling, poor circulation, loss of stamina and even cancer. The pleasure philosopher's goal, as we've noted, is to be a "healthy hedonist," not a devil-may-care death monger. Another popular drug, alcohol, acts as a stimulant initially, then as a depressant later on. However, light doses of wine, champagne or mixed drinks can relax you, open up your senses, and allow you to appreciate things that might otherwise inhibit you. A hot tub and glass of wine can be very cozy companions indeed.

One drug particularly popular in the gay culture is amyl nitrite and its variations. "Poppers," as they're called, shift blood pressure and produce unusual sensations in the body. Holding, touching and lovemaking seem intensified and

"thicker," making them popular as aphrodisiacs. Some claim poppers enhance orgasm. The real problem with amyl is that the effects are so short-lived that people abuse it over and over in one session. With moderate use, it may not be very harmful. A more destructive substance is PCP, "angel dust," a horse tranquilizer which depresses the nervous system and has been linked with violent outbursts. Cannabis (marijuana and its variations) seems to slow down and intensify sensory awareness, and some report exciting experiences with sex, massage, hot tubs, etc. Moderate use should present no major problems, but excessive use can become habituating and lead to lethargy and minor health ailments.

Another real sensory turn-on are the psychedelics, either the organic ones like peyote or magic mushrooms, or the synthetics like LSD or mescaline. These

affect the emotional centers of the brain, releasing repressed material, so they should be used with care and supervision. They intensify sense perceptions and touch to a tremendous extent. Lovemaking can seem endless and primal, and orgasms can feel absolutely out of this world. However, these drugs can turn the mind inside out and upside down, and they last up to eight hours. This supreme sensory affector exacts a stiff price in terms of endurance and psychic tumult, not to mention physical symptoms like nausea.

Nitrous oxide ("laughing gas," usually the propellant used in whipped-cream dispensers) creates a short-acting, pleasant exhilaration. Dentists often use it for anesthetic effects. MDA, a psychedeliclike compound which produces no mental distortions, enhances sensitivity for emotions and bodily feelings. During the sixties, MDA was often used to loosen inhibitions, sometimes as a stimulation for group-sex experiences. The drug is mostly used in the gay community these days.

Apart from the various effects of these substances, another harmful influence is their legal status: you can be criminally prosecuted for possession of most of them. So all facts considered, it's probably best to eschew artificial aids in your pleasure quest.

Other pleasure odds and ends include the interesting thrills that come from amusement park rides. Sliding ponds, swings and other playground activities, as well as horseback riding, also capture similar feelings. Even elevators, boats, airplanes and other fast-moving conveyances can cause such a disequilibrium, which some love. There are also new types of music designed to act on the feeling centers of the mind. Certain hypnosis tapes (often subliminal, so you can't consciously hear the instructions) can have this effect, as well as "New Age" music. One cassette, called "Astral Sounds," is reputed to produce a natural high by stimulating both sensual and sexual sensations. Of course, all gripping music affects the emotions, so it pays to explore the various types of music which provoke particular pleasure reactions in you. Dancing, which also intimately affects your emotional side, is a wonderful complement to the musical experience.

Another key pleasure pursuit that should not be neglected is self-love, better known as masturbation. You know your sexual enjoyments better than anyone else, and there's no shame in making oneself feel good. Masturbation can be a pleasant substitute when a partner is sick or unavailable. But it's also a wonderful way to learn to love and care for yourself, to exercise the fertile power of your sexual fantasies. The fantasies you dream up while masturbating may one day be tried in reality, leading to new forms of ecstasy. You'll also learn to appreciate how sexy your body is, and how capable you are of giving pleasure. Whatever you can do for yourself can also be done for another. For people inhibited about sex with others, masturbation can lessen fears and loosen blockages. It will help you appreciate your ability to give and receive sensual joy.

We've now explored pleasure from all angles—mental, physical, emotional, spiritual. It's fitting to end this chapter with a scenario for the ultimate pleasure experience. I call this the "pleasure palace," or alternatively, the "ecstasy abode," and it's not so much a physical manifestation as a fertile concept. What's involved is the creation of a space—it could be a mansion, apartment or just a private room—purely devoted to pleasure pursuits. In its most extravagant version, it could be a large house with luxurious carpeting, elegant decor, beautiful amenities, the ultimate in sound systems and creature comforts and scenic surroundings. It would be loaded with sensory delights like hot tubs, Jacuzzis, pools, water beds and tranquility tanks. The bedroom would be covered with mirrors, and fragrant aromas could be circulated at the press of a button. Massage tables would be available, as well as all massage paraphernalia.

Fine foods would be freely on hand, and the oversized bathroom would be decorated with a huge oval or heart-shaped bathtub, replete with whirlpool water jets and bubble bath solutions. Other rooms would furnish giant projector screens for watching the latest films or TV, while still others would have multimedia light panoramas to take your mind on endless voyages. Strobes, black lights, holograms, slides and perhaps a small planetarium for star-gazing would be available. Your oval-shaped bed would be suited with luxurious satin or silk sheets, and music would be pumped into the room at the touch of a button. Either robots or live help would be there to cater to your every whim and fancy. Science fiction? Not really, as all the technology already exists. What would be otherworldly is the price, since it would cost millions to put together something like this. Perhaps, however, some enterprising person will construct such a palace for rental use. A franchise chain could even be a possibility.

Even on a more modest level, there is no health resort I'm aware of which features a collection of pleasure items like hot tubs, saunas, Jacuzzis, light shows and tranquility tanks under one roof. But even if you're a student struggling to pay tuition, you can always fix up your apartment or room with as many amenities as you can comfortably afford. Or you can choose a totally simple path, just a few comfy, livable items. Pleasure is essentially an internal state, and while externals can add to one's enjoyment, the real ecstasy comes from inside. Your pleasure palace may be no more elaborate than a bedroom in which you and your favorite pleasure partner create your own pleasure dance together. On another level, the true pleasure philosopher carries his pleasure palace inside him all the time.

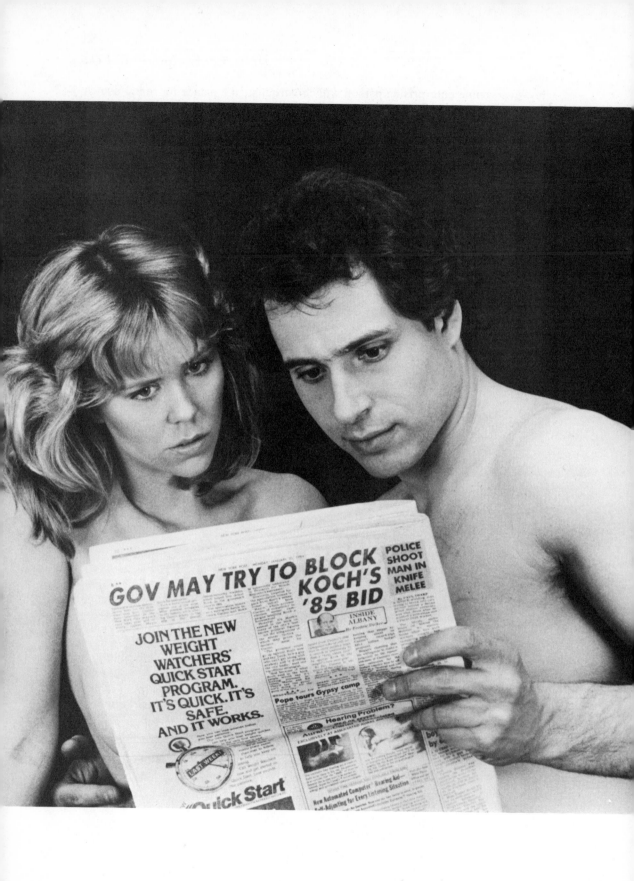

22

The Politics of Pleasure

Initially it may seem odd to be speaking about politics and pleasure in the same breath. In many respects, they seem like polar opposites. Politics brings to mind conflict, war, mudslinging, etc., while pleasure produces images of joy, fulfillment, ecstasy, peace and contentment. So what do they have to do with each other?

In the simplest sense, politics determines the type and amount of pleasure permitted in any society. The political structure of a nation is determined by many factors—including the prevailing cultural biases, social myths, economic structure—and its historical role in the world community. America is a direct cultural descendant of the Puritan ethic spawned in Europe, and this ethic is decidedly antipleasure. The Puritans, Calvinists and other hellfire preacher groups considered the body to be the repository of all evil, the representative of Satan on earth. Leading a moral life meant denying the body and its needs, not pampering and pleasuring it. Someone spouting a philosophy of ecstasy in early America might well have been burned at the stake.

And there are still powerful groups in our society who believe in this philosophy. They include the Moral Majority and most of the other TV evangelists, plus some extremely influential and affluent conservative politicians, business people and community leaders. This pervasive Puritanism has not escaped certain supposedly liberal New Age groups. For example, the predecessor to this book, *The Joy of Touch,* was banned from the shelves of one of New York's biggest New Age bookstores. Why? The manager told me the photos of the nude couple, mostly cuddling each other, "pandered to people's prurient interest." We went to great pains not to include any sexually explicit shots in that book, yet we received such a reaction from a supposedly "enlightened" individual.

The incident left an indelible impression on me, making me realize that you can just go so far in our society in trying to liberate people before powerful influences try to impose censorship. Obviously, the situation is worse in totalitarian societies like the Soviet Union, where any idea not akin to the official state line is banned. But you expect that from the Soviets, and it's a lot more shocking to see similar behavior in Western countries. I received another surprise when the Dutch edition of *The Joy of Touch* was published. They included everything in the book except the chapter on drugs, a chapter which was not only not an endorsement, but a scathing critique of the deleterious effects of most recreational chemicals. It's amazing that one cannot even objectively discuss drugs in a country with a reputation of openness and liberalism!

Fact is, freedom and pleasure are inextricable. The freer the society, the more one will be permitted to experiment. The drug laws are perhaps the most blatant example of this. Many people are afraid to expand their consciousness, and will actively persecute those who do. One example of the lengths to which they'll go is

the so-called chromosome damage studies of LSD in the sixties, studies supposedly linking the drug with deformed babies. The experiments, government-funded and media-publicized, were not only flawed, but were virtual hoaxes. It was later found that similar breakage of chromosomes would occur if you soaked them in common substances like caffeine or aspirin, but the debunking of the original "research" was never publicized. Consequently, legitimate research into the effects of these drugs was brought to a halt by public hysteria. The pleasure-killers certainly won that round.

Puritanism similarly flourishes in the sexual realm. Statute after statute forbids intercourse beyond the missionary posture between married couples. The same is true for pornographic laws. When the Commission on Obscenity and Pornography recommended legalization after careful studies, our leaders immediately renounced and condemned the report, supposedly because sexually explicit materials would "break the moral fabric of society." Interestingly, when Denmark legalized pornography in the early seventies, sales plummeted. Most of it wound up being exported to repressed countries like the U.S.

Pioneering humanistic psychologist Abraham Maslow, in his *Toward A Psychology of Being,* spent some time discussing a comparative sociology, a way of judging which social systems were most fitting for people to fulfill their potential. He felt that the best cultures were those which would allow the most needs to be filled, and those needs included self-actualization, the complete development of one's inner being. Carl Rogers, another humanistic psychologist, went even further in *Carl Rogers on Personal Power.*

In that book he frankly admitted that pursuing the humanist ideal to its ultimate was outright revolutionary. Many deeply engrained groups do not want a society of self-actualized people, but would prefer a robotized, docile population like Skinner's *Walden Two* portrays. And it's not hard to see why. Self-actualized people trust their instincts, are true to their convictions, and do not follow the herd. They are open-minded free thinkers. They're the last ones who'd go along with some Hitler-type tyrant, meaning that they'd be the first ones to go if such a figure gained power. Carl Rogers himself admits he'd be one of the first victims of a totalitarian regime.

The humanist dilemma is closely akin to that of the pleasure philosopher. Puritanical, authoritarian groups like the Moral Majority couldn't care less about your right to enjoy yourself. Instead, they prefer strict state censorship and *their right* to determine what you should read, think and feel. Pleasure philosophy is a great threat to them. After all, haven't Jerry Falwell and his fellow millionaire TV evangelists told us that God is directly guiding them as far as political affairs are concerned? And what use would a hell-fire-and-brimstone God have for pleasure?

Ironically, there's an exact opposite political tendency which equally threatens the bliss-seeker. This mainly comes from Madison Avenue and the Lords of Finance, who are most interested in turning you upside down and shaking your money loose. Most of them are completely amoral and unethical; they just want to sell you their wares and say good-bye. In some respect, they act as a check on Moral Majority types, because the Madison Avenue whiz kids will fight any attempts to keep them from selling their products. Problem is, most of the things they're hawking are purely pseudopleasure items, some of which are downright destructive.

Just a few of their big money-makers include booze, tobacco, large or fast cars and legal drugs. Many of these products are not only harmful, but they mask problems which you'd otherwise have to cope with and overcome. Feel inadequate? Try racing down the street in a souped-up sports car and that'll give you a sense of power. In a bad mood? Booze, Valium or aspirin can always take care of that. Want to relax? Light up a cigarette.

Even the more benign money-makers burn up your time and cash so you don't develop discriminating pleasure sensibilities. Think of the hours wasted on mindless TV fare, trashy movies, idiotic arcade games and the like. The values the admen put out are also pure pseudopleasure: conform, look like everyone else, keep up with the Joneses, *ad nauseam.* "Dress for success" is one of their big themes, making you feel out of place if you don't wear the right business wardrobe or designer clothes.

These values promote feelings of inadequacy rather than self-actualization. If you follow your own drummer, you may be left out in the cold. These are very strong cultural pressures, and almost impossible to escape. The messages of mindless obedience and conformity are not only reinforced in the media, but at work. If the Thirteenth Amendment had not abolished slavery, it really would not surprise me to see people entering into work contracts that would include a master/slave arrangement. Although unspoken, many work settings are not that different, and neither are many marriages. The recent spate of palimony suits may be testimony to this. The woman tells the court that she had a verbal contract to provide domestic and sexual services, and now she expects payment for same. This is about as removed from love as is imaginable.

THE PLEASURE BOOK

The tone of this book to this point has basically been celebratory, so the present criticism may seem startling. However, before ending, I want to point out some of the implications of fully following the pleasure philosophy. "Having a good time" may seem like an idea agreeable to all, but when you start to explore peak experiences of pleasure, you may run into some problems. There are certain "pleasure principles" and these include boldness, standing up for one's rights, living up to one's potential, seeking novel experiences, taking risks, being socially concerned and seeking ecstasy, among others, that threaten people who are satisfied with leading the life of contented cows. My final advice is not to allow them to discourage you. Mystic philosopher Carlos Castaneda, whom I had the rare privilege of studying under, used to tell us to follow the "Path with Heart," the road that appeals to your instincts. This means thinking for yourself, being your own person, not falling for the cowardly entreaties of beaten souls. The Pleasure Philosophy is definitely a Path with Heart, and I hope you pursue it to the fullest.

This bibliography/reference list is one of the most significant parts of the book. In it you will find leads to all the material covered in the text. *The Pleasure Book* should be viewed as only the start of your search for ecstasy. The areas in the text that puzzle you, the references you may want to track down, the tools to lead to further discovery will all be found here in this bibliography. Here I am offering you the vast resources of a career which few could duplicate before age thirty-five.

Beyond my formal academic training in psychology, law and journalism, my business background offers an added wealth of information to be shared. I have written a book on the occult, studied with mystic Carlos Castaneda, edited a UFO magazine and a management newsletter, written for men's magazines, business publications and have been a newspaper reporter. As an attorney, I worked on Wall Street, and won cases for the Securities and Exchange Commission and U.S. Attorney's Office. I served for six months as Dean of Living Ministries International College, during which time I achieved formal ministerial credentials. I've also taught courses on love, sorcery, healing and the singles lifestyle. Most recently, I passed the Mensa IQ test and the mutual funds dealer exam for the National Association of Securities Dealers.

I've used my own life as an experimental ground to put into action the pleasure philosophy. This bibliography represents the best materials I've come across on each respective area covered. In order not to overwhelm the reader, I've limited each topic to those books which I feel are particularly valuable. In most cases, when I've left out some particularly popular books, it's not because I'm unaware of them, but because I've thoroughly scrutinized them and feel the information is misleading, wrong or even detrimental to the reader's development. You can count on the quality of the publications in this bibliography. In some cases in which I felt some special explanation was needed about a particular book, I've added some short comments in parentheses.

The list closes with a bibliography of the best audiotape and other nonprint programs I'm aware of. These cover all areas in the book, including love, spiritual development, prosperity, success, inspiration and every conceivable area of learning. As the text indicates, tape learning is one of the most practical, as well as powerful, ways of obtaining new information. Ordering information has been included for your convenience.

So there you have it. You can use this list to explore in greater depth virtually any ecstasy experience imaginable, and expand your horizons just as far as you see fit. In closing, I'd like to indicate that those of you wishing to comment on *The Pleasure Book,* or interested in subscribing to a new pleasure/hedonist newsletter which will continually update *The Pleasure Book,* can contact me via Human Services Unlimited, P.O. Box 81, Staten Island, NY 10301. I wish you all peace and the most pleasurable life possible!

BIBLIOGRAPHY

1. BOOKS AND ARTICLES
The Psychology of Pleasure

Freud, Sigmund. *Beyond the Pleasure Principle.* Norton, New York 1961
Freud, Sigmund. *Civilization and Its Discontents.* Norton, New York 1962
Marcuse, Herbert. *Eros and Civilization.* Vintage, New York 1955
Masters, William and Virginia Johnson. *The Pleasure Bond.* Bantam, New York 1976
Rueger, Russ. *The Joy of Touch.* Simon & Schuster, New York 1981
Rueger, Russ. *The Pleasure Book.* Gallery Press, New York 1973

Peak Experiences and Self-Actualization

Dyer, Wayne. *The Sky's the Limit.* Simon & Schuster, New York 1980
Maslow, Abraham. *The Farther Reaches of Human Nature.* Penguin, New York 1971
Maslow, Abraham. *Toward a Psychology of Being.* Van Nostrand, New York 1968
May, Rollo. *Psychology and the Human Dilemma.* Norton, New York 1979
Rogers, Carl. *Carl Rogers on Personal Power.* Dell, New York 1977
Rogers, Carl. *On Becoming a Person.* Houghton Mifflin, Boston 1961

Pleasure Prohibitions

Freud, Sigmund. *Civilization and Its Discontents.* Norton, New York 1962
Marcuse, Herbert. *Eros and Civilization.* Vintage, New York 1955
Rueger, Russ. "Obscenity, the Case for Free Speech," in *Obscenity: Censorship or Free Choice?* Greenleaf, San Diego 1971
Rueger, Russ. "The Shunned Sense," *Contact,* December 1982/January 1983

The Pleasure Philosophy

Rueger, Russ. "The Art of Erotic Tickling," *Gallery,* October 1976
Rueger, Russ. "8 Ways to Win and Keep a Super-Beautiful Woman," *Gallery,* August 1980
Rueger, Russ. "The Joy of Anomie," *Human Behavior,* July 1974
Rueger, Russ. "Making Her Fall In Love With You," *Gallery's Guide to Great Loving.* Gallery Press, New York 1983
Rueger, Russ. "Never Pick a Woman Up by Her Ears," *Gallery,* September 1983
Rueger, Russ. "The Sensuous Art of Cuddling," *Penthouse,* August 1973
Rueger, Russ. "Sexy Friendships," *Gallery,* June 1982
Rueger, Russ. "Smooth Talk, 80s Style," *Gallery,* June 1983
Rueger, Russ. "Skin Hunger," *Contact,* June/July 1983

Mental Pleasure

Allen, James. *As A Man Thinketh.* DeVorss, Marina del Rey, CA
Besant, Annie & C. W. Leadbeater. *Thought Forms.* Theosophical Publishing House, Adyar 1925 (highly occult)
Bristol, Claude. *The Magic of Believing.* Cornerstone, New York 1975
Eikerenkoetter, Frederick. *Rev. Ike's Secrets for Health, Happiness and Prosperity.* Science of Living, New York (spiritual approach)
Hill, Napolean and W. Clement Stone. *Success Through a Positive Mental Attitude.* Pocket, New York 1977
Gawain, Shakti. *Creative Visualization.* Whatever, Mill Valley, CA 1978
Holmes, Ernest. *The Science of Mind.* Dodd, Mead, New York, 1938
Keyes, Ken. *Handbook to Higher Consciousness.* Living Love, Berkeley 1975
Maltz, Maxwell. *Psychocybernetics.* Prentice-Hall, Englewood Cliffs, NJ 1960

Orr, Leonard & Sondra Ray. *Rebirthing in the New Age.* Celestial Arts, Millbrae, CA 1977

Peale, Norman Vincent. *The Amazing Results of Positive Thinking.* Fawcett, Greenwich, CN 1959

Peale, Norman Vincent. *The Power of Positive Thinking.* Prentice-Hall, Englewood Cliffs, NJ 1956

Ponder, Catherine. *The Dynamic Laws of Prosperity.* Prentice-Hall, Englewood Cliffs, NJ 1962

Schwartz, David. *The Magic of Thinking Big.* Cornerstone, New York 1965

Silva, Jose. *The Silva Mind Control Method.* Pocket, New York 1977

Subramuniya, Master. *The Power of Affirmation.* Comstock House, San Francisco, 1973

Szekely, Edmond. *The Art of Study.* Academy Books, San Diego 1973

Szekely, Edmond. *Books: Our Eternal Companions.* Academy of Creative Living, San Diego, 1971

Troward, Thomas. *The Creative Process in the Individual.* Dodd, Mead, New York 1915

Troward, Thomas. *The Edinburgh Lectures on Mental Science.* Dodd, Mead, New York 1909

Work

Blanchard, Kenneth and Spencer Johnson. *The One Minute Manager.* Morrow, New York 1982

Cohen, Peter. *The Gospel According to the Harvard Business School.* Penguin, New York 1973

Ewing, David. *Freedom Inside the Organization.* E. P. Dutton, New York, 1977

Fairchild, Roy, ed. *Humanizing the Workplace.* Prometheus, Buffalo, 1974

Feinberg, Mortimer et al. *The New Psychology for Managing People.* Prentice-Hall, Englewood Cliffs, NJ 1975

Gartner, Michael, ed. *The Road to the Top.* Dow Jones, Princeton, 1970

Greiff, Barrie and Preston Munter. *Tradeoffs: Executive, Family and Organizational Life.* NAL, New York 1980

Jencks, Christopher. *Who Gets Ahead?* Basic, New York 1979

Kerr, Clark *et al. Work in America.* Van Nostrand, New York 1979

Law, Sylvia. *The Rights of the Poor.* Avon, New York 1974

Maccoby, Michael. *The Gamesman.* Bantam, New York 1978

Margolis, Diane. *The Managers: Corporate Life in America.* Morrow, New York 1979

Pollock, Ted. *Moving On Up.* Hawthorn, New York 1979

Rueger, Russ. "Dangerous Currents," *Connektions,* September 1983 (Economic trends and theories)

Rueger, Russ. "The One Minute Manager," *Connektions,* November 1983 (Review of recent management theories and techniques)

Siu, R. G. H. *Transcending the Power Game: The Way to Executive Serenity.* Wiley, New York 1980

Terkel, Studs. *Working.* Avon, New York 1975

Weber, Max. *The Protestant Ethic and the Spirit of Capitalism.* Scribners, New York 1958

Westin, Alan and Stephan Salisbury, eds. *Individual Rights in the Corporation.* Pantheon, New York 1980

Success and Achievement

Allen, James. *Freedom and Truth.* Successful Achievement, Lexington 1971

Bremer, Sidney. *Successful Achievement,* 4 Vols. Successful Achievement, Lexington 1971

Bermont, Hubert. *How to Become a Successful Consultant in Your Own Field.* Bermont Books, Washington, D.C. 1978

Blotnick, Srully. *Getting Rich Your Own Way.* Doubleday, New York 1980

BIBLIOGRAPHY

Butterworth, Eric. *Spiritual Economics.* Unity Press, Unity Village, MO 1983
Franklin, Benjamin. *The Autobiography of Benjamin Franklin.* Pocket, New York 1938
Gifford, J. Nebraska *et al. Secrets of Success.* Pocket, New York 1980
Gillies, Jerry. *Moneylove.* Evans, New York 1978
Hill, Napolean. *Think and Grow Rich.* Wilshire, North Hollywood 1966
Jordan, William. *The Power of Peace.* Successful Achievement, Lexington 1971
Keyes, Ken and Bruce Burkan. *How to Make Your Life Work.* Living Love, St. Mary, KY 1974
Keyes, Ken. *Taming Your Mind.* Living Love, St. Mary, KY 1975
Lakein, Alan. *How to Get Control of Your Time and Life.* Signet, New York 1973
LeBoeuf, Michael. *Working Smart.* McGraw-Hill, New York 1979
Mandino, Og. *The Greatest Salesman in the World.* Bantam, New York 1981
Mandino, Og. *The Greatest Success in the World.* Bantam, New York 1981
Marden, Orison. *Good Cheer and Prosperity.* Successful Achievement, Lexington 1971
Rueger, Russ. "The Successful Singles Lifestyle," *Singles Plus,* June 1983
Rueger, Russ. "Scholarly Thoughts," *Student Lawyer,* February 1981
Sarlat, Noah, ed. *How I Made A Million.* Paperback Library, New York 1961
Winston, Stephanie. *Getting Organized.* Norton, New York 1978 (Also see references in section on *Work*)

Friendship

Cooley, Charles. *Human Nature and the Social Order.* Schocken, New York 1964
Dyer, Wayne. *Your Erroneous Zones.* Avon, New York 1976
Dyer, Wayne. *Pulling Your Own Strings.* Avon, New York 1977
Frieze, Irene *et al. Women and Sex Roles.* Norton, New York 1978
Fromm, Erich. *Man For Himself.* Fawcett, Greenwich, CN 1947
Gans, Herbert. *The Levittowners.* Vintage, New York 1967
Goffman, Erving. *The Presentation of Self in Everyday Life.* Anchor, New York 1959
Heider, Fritz. *The Psychology of Interpersonal Relations.* Wiley, New York 1958
Josephson, Eric and Mary. *Man Alone: Alienation in Modern Society.* Dell, New York 1962
Katz, Elihu and Paul Lazarsfeld. *Personal Influence.* Free Press, Glencoe 1955
Laing, R. D. *Self and Others.* Pantheon, New York 1969
Lang, Doe. *The Charisma Book.* Wyden, New York 1980
Liebow, Elliot. *Tally's Corner.* Little, Brown, Boston 1967
Marden, Orison. *Friendship.* Successful Achievement, Lexington 1961
O'Neill, John. *Sociology as a Skin Trade.* Harper, New York 1972
Mead, George. *Mind Self & Society.* Phoenix, Chicago 1967
Rueger, Russ. "Dodging Double Standard Snags," *Gallery,* February 1982
Rueger, Russ. "Seeking Freedom from the Male Myth," *Human Behavior,* April 1973
Rueger, Russ. "Sexy Friendships," *Gallery,* June 1982
Rueger, Russ. "The Successful Singles Lifestyle," *Singles Plus,* June 1983
Schmitt, Richard. *Martin Heidegger on Being Human.* Random House, New York 1969
Slater, Philip. *The Pursuit of Loneliness.* Beacon, Boston 1970
Steiner, Calude. *Scripts People Live.* Grove, New York 1974
Tagiuri, Renato and Luigi Petrullo. *Person Perception and Inter-Personal Behavior.* Stanford University Press, Stanford, CA 1958
Toch, Hans and Henry Smith. *Social Perception.* Van Nostrand, Princeton 1968
Wallace, Anthony. *Culture and Personality.* Random House, New York 1961
Whyte, William. *Street Corner Society.* University of Chicago, Chicago 1955

Love

Anonymous. *A Course in Miracles,* 3 Vols. Foundation for Inner Peace, New York 1977
Butterworth, Eric. *Life is for Loving.* Harper, New York 1973

Colgrove, Melba *et al. How to Survive the Loss of a Love.* Bantam, New York 1976

Donnelly, Doris. *Learning to Forgive.* Macmillan, New York 1979

Eibl-Eibesfeldt. *Love and Hate.* Holt, New York 1972

Fortune, Dion. *Esoteric Philosophy of Love and Marriage.* Aquarian Press, Wellingborough, Northamptonshire, England 1974

Fromm, Erich. *The Art of Loving.* Bantam, New York 1956

Fromme, Alan. *The Ability to Love.* Pocket, New York 1965

Jampolsky, Gerald. *Love is Letting Go of Fear.* Bantam, New York 1979

Keyes, Ken. *A Conscious Person's Guide to Relationships.* Living Love, St. Mary, KY 1979

Keyes, Ken. *How to Enjoy Your Life In Spite of It All.* Living Love, St. Mary, KY 1980

Keyes, Ken. *Prescriptions for Happiness.* Living Love, St. Mary, KY 1980

Money, John. *Love & Love Sickness.* Johns Hopkins University Press, Baltimore 1980

Ponder, Catherine. *The Prospering Power of Love.* Unity Press, Unity Village, MO 1966

Ray, Ann. *Journey into Light.* University of the Trees Press, Boulder Creek, CA 1977 (Touching story of a woman's struggle with love and spiritual growth)

Ray, Sondra. *I Deserve Love.* Les Femmes, Millbrae, CA 1976

Ray, Sondra. *Loving Relationships.* Celestial Arts, Millbrae, CA 1980

Rueger, Russ. "Beating Your Love Rivals" in *The Pleasure Book.* Gallery Press, New York 1973

Rueger, Russ. "The Fine Art of Breaking Up," *Gallery,* April 1982

Rueger, Russ. "Making Her Fall in Love with You," *Gallery's Guide to Great Loving.* Gallery Press, New York 1983

Rueger, Russ. "Never Pick A Woman Up by Her Ears," *Gallery,* September 1982

Rueger, Russ. "Smooth Talk, '80s Style," *Gallery,* April 1983

Schickel, Richard. *Singled Out.* Viking, New York 1981 (For those just returning to single life)

Shinn, Florence. *The Game of Life.* Cornerstone, New York 1925

Sonenblick, Jerry. *The Legality of Love.* Jove, New York 1981

Strabo, Mikhail and Lynn Archer. *Love.* Guidance House, New York 1945

Watts, Alan. *Nature, Man & Woman.* Vintage, New York 1970

Weber, Eric and Judi Miller. *The Shy Person's Guide to Love and Loving.* Times Books, New York 1979

The Healthy Hedonist

Andrews, Valerie. *The Psychic Power of Running.* Rawson, New York 1978

Ballentine, Rudolph. *Diet & Nutrition: A Holistic Approach.* Himalayan Institute, Honesdale, PA 1978

Bennett, Arnold. *How to Live on 24 Hours A Day.* Cornerstone, New York 1962

De Langre, Jacques. *Do-in 2: The Ancient Art of Rejuvenation Through Self-Massage.* Happiness Press, Magalia, CA 1974

Health Policy Advisory Center. *The American Health Empire: Power, Profits and Politics.* Vintage, New York 1971

Kalson, Stanley. *Holistic H.E.L.P. Handbook.* International Holistic Center 1981 (Diet, exercise, meditation, etc.)

Kloss, Jethro. *Back to Eden.* Benedict Lust, New York 1981 (Herbology)

Kulvinskas, Viktoras. *Survival Into the 21st Century—Planetary Healers Manual.* Omangod Press, Woodstock Valley, CT 1975 (Exercise, yoga, natural foods, etc.)

Pembrook, Linda. *How to Beat Fatigue.* Avon, New York 1975

Popenoe, Chris. *Wellness* Yes!, Washington, D.C. 1977 (Annotated bibliography on all areas of health)

Pyle, Irving. *The New American Medicine Show.* Unity Press, Santa Cruz, CA 1979

Rama, Swami *et al. Science of Breath.* Himalayan Institute, Honesdale, PA 1979

Ray, Sondra. *The Only Diet There Is.* Celestial Arts, Millbrae, CA 1981 (Spiritual approach to dieting)

Sharper Image Catalog (San Francisco; this and similar catalogs provide late-breaking news on high-tech home exercise items)

Sheehan, George. *Dr. Sheehan on Running.* Bantam, New York 1975

Shurtleff, William and Akiko Aoyagi. *The Book of Tofu.* Ballantine, New York 1979 (Complete recipes for high-protein health product)

Szekely, Edmond. *Biogenic Fulfillment: The Tender Touch.* Academy Books, San Diego 1977 (Ancient Essene modes of nutrition and rejuvenation)

Szekely, Edmond. *The Essene Science of Fasting.* International Biogenic Society, Cartago, Costa Rica 1981

Szekely, Edmond. *The Essene Science of Life.* Academy Books, San Diego 1976. (Ancient principles of diet and fitness)

Spino, Mike. *Beyond Jogging.* Berkley, New York 1977

Stearn, Jess. *Yoga, Youth and Reincarnation.* Doubleday, New York 1965

Whole Life Times, Diet and Health Times and similar publications found in health food stores

Wilhelm, Tim & Glenda. *The Bicycle Touring Book: The Complete Guide to Bicycle Recreation.* Rodale Press, Emmaus, PA 1980

Zimardi, Ron. *Inside Out: A Spiritual Manual for Prison Life.* Hanuman Foundation, New York 1976 (Excellent guide to yoga, meditation, etc.)

Recreation and Relaxation

Ajaya, Swami. *Yoga Psychology: A Practical Guide to Meditation.* Himalayan Institute, Honesdale, PA 1976

Albury, Paul. *Story of the Bahamas.* MacMillan, London 1975 (Excellent example of a vacation guidebook)

Arya, Pandit. *Superconscious Meditation.* Himalayan Institute, Honesdale, PA 1978

Benson, Herbert. *The Relaxation Response.* Morrow, New York 1975

Caprio, Frank and Joseph Berger. *Helping Yourself With Self-Hypnosis.* Prentice-Hall, Englewood Cliffs, NJ 1963

Dass, Ram. *Be Here Now.* Lama Foundation, San Cristobal, NM 1971 (Wide-ranging guide to yoga, meditation and spirituality)

Ebon, Martin. *The Relaxation Controversy.* Signet, New York 1976 (A comparison of different methods)

Goldstein, Joseph. *The Experience of Insight.* Unity Press, Santa Cruz, CA 1976 (Buddhist meditation)

Govinda, Lama. *Creative Meditation and Multi-Dimensional Consciousness.* Theosophical Pub. House, Wheaton, IL 1976

Green, Elmer & Alice. *Beyond Biofeedback.* Dell, New York 1977 (New technologies of relaxation and beyond)

Hammel, Faye. *Arthur Frommer's Guide to Boston.* Frommer/Pasmantier Publishing Co., New York 1979 (These and similar guides are excellent for vacation planning)

Hidalgo, Alberto and Jack Gray. *How to Hypnotize.* Borden Pub. Co., Alhambra, CA 1966

Kerouac, Jack. *On the Road.* Signet, New York 1957 (Zany fictional account of cross-country journey)

McWilliams, Peter. *The TM Program: A Basic Handbook.* Fawcett, Greenwich, CT 1976

Jesus and Kuthumi. *Prayer and Meditation.* Summit, Malibu, CA 1978

Peo, Scandinavian Yoga and Meditationschool. *Medical & Psychological Scientific Research on Yoga & Meditation.* Peo, etc. Denmark 1978

Russell, Jerry & Renny. *On the Loose.* Ballantine, New York 1967 (Wonderful account of free-spirited journey in the great outdoors)

Selye, Hans. *Stress Without Distress.* Signet, New York 1974
Teplitz, Jerry and Shelly Kellman. *How to Relax and Enjoy.* Japan Publications, Tokyo 1977 (Concise instructions on shiatsu, nutrition, yoga, relaxation, etc.)
(Also see references in preceding section, such as *The Bicycle Touring Book.*)

Bodywork

Carter, Ruth. *Hand Reflexology.* Parker, West Nyack, NY 1975
Carter, Ruth. *Helping Yourself with Foot Reflexology.* Parker, West Nyack, NY 1969
De Langre, Jacques. *Do-in 2: The Ancient Art of Rejuvenation Through Self-Massage.* Happiness Press, Magalia, CA 1978
Eden, Jerome. *Orgone Energy.* Exposition, Hicksville, NY 1972
Kurtz, Ron and Hector Prestera. *The Body Reveals.* Harper, New York 1976
Kulvinskas, Viktoras. *Survival Into the 21st Century—Planetary Healers Manual.* Oman-god Press, Woodstock Valley, CT 1975 (Good discussion of reflexology and shiatsu)
Mann, Felix. *Acupuncture.* Vintage, New York 1973
Ohashi, Mataru. *Ohashi's Chart.* Shiatsu Education Center of America, New York (Illustrates acupressure points and meridians)
Oliver, William. *New Body Reflexology.* Bi-World, Provo, Utah 1976
Reich, Wilhelm. *The Mass Psychology of Fascism.* Farrar, New York 1969
Rueger, Russ. "Reflexology Massage," "Shiatsu," and "Bodywork" chapters in *The Joy of Touch.* Simon & Schuster, New York 1981
Schultz, William. *Shiatsu: Japanese Finger Pressure.* Bell, New York 1976
Serizawa, Katsusuke. *Massage: The Oriental Method.* Japan Publications, Tokyo 1980
Teplitz, Jerry and Shelly Kellman. *How to Relax and Enjoy.* Japan Publications, Tokyo 1977 (Good discussion of shiatsu)
(*Whole Life Times, International Journal of Holistic Health and Medicine, New Age* and similar publications often carry stories on bodywork)

The Beauty Quest

Abel, Dominick. *Guide to the Wines of the United States.* Cornerstone, New York 1979
Anonymous. *Course in Miracles,* 3 Vols. Foundation for Inner Peace, New York 1977
Blanshard, Paul. *Classics of Free Thought.* Prometheus, Buffalo, 1977
Brande, Dorothea. *Becoming a Writer.* Tarcher, Los Angeles 1934
Butterworth, Eric. *Life is for Loving.* Harper, New York 1973
Casey, Douglas. *The International Man.* Kephart, Alexandria, VA 1978
Cirino, Robert. *Don't Blame the People: How the News Media Use Bias, Distortion and Censorship to Manipulate Public Opinion.* Vintage, New York 1972
Craven, Thomas. *A Treasury of Art Masterpieces.* Simon & Schuster, New York 1958
Enright, Evelyn and Ann Larsen. *Decorating Ideas for the Active Rooms.* Armstrong, Lancaster, PA 1967
Finch, Christopher. *Pop Art.* E. P. Dutton, New York 1968
French, Charles. *1981 Guide to U.S. Coins.* Cornerstone, New York 1977
Fromm, Erich. *Fear of Freedom.* Routledge, London 1960
Henry, Jules. *Culture Against Man.* Vintage, New York 1963
Huizinga, Johan. *Homo Ludens.* Beacon, Boston 1955 (Play instinct)
Kurtz, Paul. *Exuberance.* Wilshire, North Hollywood, CA
Lippard, Lucy. *Changing Essays in Art Criticism.* E. P. Dutton, New York 1971
Marcuse, Herbert. *One-Dimensional Man.* Beacon, Boston 1966
Mills, C. Wright. *The Sociological Imagination.* Oxford, New York 1959
Molloy, John. *Dress for Success.* Warner, New York 1975
Piaget, Jean. *The Child's Conception of the World.* Littlefield, Totowa, NJ 1967

Popenoe, Chris. *Inner Development.* Yes! Washington, D.C. 1979 (Annotated bibliography of books for inner growth)

Racz, Rhonda. *101 Great Decorating Ideas.* Bantam, New York 1969

Radcliffe-Brown, A.AR. *Structure and Function in Primitive Society.* Free Press, New York 1965

Radio Shack. *Electronics Data Book.* Radio Shack, Fort Worth 1972

Rueger, Russ. "8 Ways to Win and Keep a Super-Beautiful Woman," *Gallery,* August 1980

Russell, Jerry & Renny. *On the Loose.* Ballantine, New York 1967

Signature Magazine (Diner's Club card publication; this and similar magazines are stocked with articles about travel and the good life)

Torrance, Paul. *The Search for Satori and Creativity.* Creative Education Foundation, Buffalo, NY 1979

Warshow, Robert. *The Immediate Experience: Movies, Comics, Theatre and Other Aspects of Popular Culture.* Anchor, New York 1964

Williams, Oscar and Edwin Honig, eds. *The Mentor Book of Major American Poets.* Mentor, New York 1962

(Also see books in section on peak experiences and self-actualization)

Psychic Pleasure

Davis, A. R. and W. C. Rawls. *The Magnetic Effect.* Exposition, Hicksville, NY 1975

Davis, A. R. and W. C. Rawls. *Magnetism and its Effects on the Living System.* Exposition, Hicksville, NY 1974

Davis, A. R. and W. C. Rawls. *The Rainbow in Your Hands.* Exposition, Hicksville, NY 1976

Eden, Jerome. *Animal Magnetism and the Life Force.* Exposition, Hicksville, NY 1974

Gordon, Richard. *Your Healing Hands.* Unity Press, Santa Cruz, CA 1978

Hills, Christopher. *Into Meditation Now.* University of the Trees Press, Boulder Creek, CA 1979 (Good discussion on chakras)

Krieger, Dolores. *The Therapeutic Touch.* Prentice-Hall, Englewood Cliffs, NJ 1979

Miller, Roberta. *Psychic Massage.* Harper, New York 1975

Ostrander, Sheila and Lynn Shroeder. *Psychic Discoveries Behind the Iron Curtain.* Bantam, New York 1971

Ramacharaka, Yogi. *Fourteen Lessons in Yogi Philosophy.* Yogi Publication Society, Chicago 1931

Ramacharaka, Yogi. *Psychic Healing.* Yogi Publication Society, Chicago 1931

Rueger, Russ. "Psychic Healing" in *The Joy of Touch.* Simon & Schuster, New York 1981

Spiritual Pleasure

(See also references in Mental Pleasure section)

Allen, James. *Secrets of Success* (cassette tape)

Anonymous. *Course in Miracles.* Foundation for Inner Peace, New York 1977

Anonymous. *The Forgotten Books of Eden.* Crown, New York 1980

Anonymous. *The Impersonal Life.* Devorss, Marina del Rey, CA 1981

Arya, Pandit. *God.* Himalayan Institute, Honesdale, PA 1979

Arya, Pandit. *Meditation and the Art of Dying.* Himalayan Institute, Honesdale, PA 1979

Budge, E. A. Wallis. *Egyptian Magic.* Dover, New York 1971

Butler, W. E. *Magic and the Qabalah.* Acquarian, Northamptonshire, England 1978

Cady, H. Emilie. *Lessons in Truth.* Unity Press, Unity Village, MO

Chilson, Richard. *I Can Pray, You Can Pray.* McKay, New York 1978

Dass, Hari Baba. *Hariakhan Baba, Known, Unknown.* Sri Rama Foundation, Savis, CA 1975 (Story of immortal yogi saint of Himalayas)

Dass, Ram. *Grist for the Mill.* Unity Press, Santa Cruz, CA 1977

Dass, Ram. *The Only Dance There Is.* Anchor, New York 1974

Denning, Melita & Osborne Phillips. *The Magical Philosophy,* 5 Vols. Llewellyn Publications, St. Paul, MN 1981

Fromm, Erich. *Psychoanalysis and Religion.* Bantam, New York 1972

Fromm, Erich. *You Shall Be As Gods.* Fawcett, New York 1966

Golas, Thaddeus. *The Lazy Man's Guide to Enlightenment.* Bantam, New York 1980

Harner, Michael. *Way of the Shaman.* Bantam, New York 1980

Hopkins, Emma Curtis. *High Mysticism.* DeVorss, Santa Monica, CA 1974

Humphreys, Christmas. *Buddhism.* Penguin, Baltimore 1951

Humphreys, Christmas. *Zen Buddhism.* Unwin, London 1963

James, William. *The Varieties of Religious Experience.* NAL, New York 1958

Muktananda, Swami. *Play of Consciousness.* Harper, San Francisco 1978

Oxford Univ. Press. *Lost Books of the Bible.* Bell, New York 1979

Oxford Univ. Press. *The New Scofield Reference Bible.* Oxford, New York 1967

Prabhavananda, Swami and C. Isherwood. *The Song of God: Bhagavad-Gita.* Mentor, New York 1951

Prophet, Mark L. *Cosmic Consciousness.* Summit, Malibu, CA 1981

Prophet, Mark L. *Understanding Yourself: Doorway to the Superconscious.* Summit, Malibu, CA 1981

Ramacharaka, Yogi. *Advance Course in Yogi Philosophy and Oriental Occultism.* Yogi Publication Society, Chicago 1931

Ramacharaka, Yogi. *Lessons in Gnani Yoga.* Yogi Publication Society, Chicago 1934

Ramacharaka, Yogi. *Raja Yoga.* Yogi Publication Society, Chicago 1934

Scholem, Gershom. *On the Kabbalah and Its Symbolism.* Schocken, New York 1969

Smith, Adam. *Powers of Mind.* Random House, New York 1975

Spalding, Baird. *Life & Teachings of the Masters of the Far East,* 5 Vols. DeVorss, Marina del Rey, CA 1955

Starhawk. *The Spiral Dance.* Harper, San Francisco 1979 (Pagan rituals)

Szekely, Edmond. *The Essene Gospel of Peace,* Books One—Four. International Biogenic Society, Orosi, Costa Rica 1981

Teutsch, Joel Marie and Champion K. Teutsch. *From Here to Greater Happiness.* Price, Los Angeles 1975

Tillich, Paul. *Dynamics of Faith.* Harper, New York 1958

Tzu, Lao. *The Way of Life.* Mentor, New York 1955 (Taoism)

Waite, A. E. *Lamps of Western Mysticism.* Rudolf Steiner Pubs., Blauvelt, NY 1973

Watts, Alan. *The Book On the Taboo Against Knowing Who You Are.* Collier, New York 1967

Watts, Alan. *The Way of Zen.* Mentor, New York 1957

Yogananda, Paramahansa. *Autobiography of a Yogi.* Self-Realization Fellowship, Los Angeles 1979

Zaehner, R. C. *Mysticism, Sacred and Profane.* Oxford, New York 1961

Sensual Pleasure—Touch

Colton, Helen. *The Gift of Touch.* Putnam, New York 1983

Curtis, Patricia. "Animals are good for the handicapped, perhaps all of us," *Smithsonian,* July 1981

Downing, George. *The Massage Book.* Random House, New York 1972

Hofer, Jack. *Total Massage.* Grosset & Dunlap, New York 1977

Inkeles, Gordon. *The New Massage.* Putnam, New York 1980

Jackson, Jim, producer. "Man's Best Medicine," *60 Minutes.* CBS TV Network, aired October 3, 1982 (Therapeutic benefits from pets)

Levy, Ronald. *I Can Only Touch You Now.* Prentice-Hall, Englewood Cliffs, NJ 1973

BIBLIOGRAPHY

Montagu, Ashley. *Touching: the Human Significance of the Skin.* Harper, New York 1971
Morris, Desmond. *Intimate Behaviour.* Random House, New York 1971
NOVA, "A Touch of Sensitivity," aired on PBS December 9, 1980
Rueger, Russ. "The Art of Erotic Tickling," *Gallery,* October 1976
Rueger, Russ. "The Joy of Touch," *Gallery,* September 1981
Rueger, Russ. *The Joy of Touch.* Simon & Schuster, New York 1981
Rueger, Russ. "The Sensuous Art of Cuddling," *Penthouse,* August 1973
Rueger, Russ. "The Shunned Sense," *Contact,* December 1982/January 1983
Rueger, Russ. "Skin Hunger," *Contact,* June/July 1983
Simon, Sidney. *Caring, Feeling, Touching.* Argus, Niles, IL 1978
Weber, E. H. *The Sense of Touch.* Academic Press, New York 1978
Wylder, Joseph. *Psychic Pets: The Secret World of Animals.* Harper, New York 1978
Zerinsky, Sidney. *The Swedish Massage Work Book.* Swedish Institute, New York 1975

Sensual Pleasure—Other Senses

Caswell-Massey Catalog, New York (Oils, soaps, cosmetics, fragrances, perfumes, colognes, incense, creams, etc.)
Engen, Trygg. "Why the Aroma Lingers on," *Psychology Today,* May 1980 (Sense of smell)
Frazier, Gregory and Beverly. *The Bath Book.* Troubador Press, San Francisco 1973
Gunther, Bernard. *Sense Relaxation.* Macmillan, New York 1968 (Multisensory exercises)
Krijn, Vera. *The Sheraton World Cookbook.* Bobbs-Merrill, New York 1982 (Cookbooks are excellent ways to develop gourmet tastes)
Maclay, K. T. *Total Beauty Catalog.* Coward, New York 1978
Rama, Swami, *et al. The Science of Breath.* Himalayan Institute, Honesdale, PA 1979 (sense of smell)
Rosen, Lillie. "Nancy Milano and the Joy of Creative Piano Study," *Wisdoms Child New York Guide,* November 14, 1983 (Music appreciation)
Sharper Image Catalog, San Francisco; *Hammacher Schlemmer* Catalog, New York. (Catalogs like these offer the latest in sensory gadgets, high-tech and otherwise)
Signature magazine (Diner's Club Card holder's publication. These and similar magazines offer the latest in sensory stimulation data.)
Stubbs, Ray. "The Tasty Art of Oral Massage," *Forum International,* 1981 (Creams, syrups, sauces and sex)
Van Dyke, Grace. "Sensuous Scents," *Gallery,* November 1982
Villee, Claude. *Biology.* Saunders, Philadelphia 1964

Sexual Attitudes

Altman, Carole. "The Grafenberg Spot," *Gallery's Guide to Great Loving.* Gallery Press, New York 1973
Bengis, Ingrid. *Combat in the Erogenous Zones.* Bantam, New York 1973
Bernard, Jessie. *The Sex Game.* Prentice-Hall, Englewood Cliffs, NJ 1968
Fasteau, Marc. *The Male Machine.* McGraw-Hill, New York 1973
Firestone, Shulamith. *The Dialectic of Sex.* Bantam, New York 1972
Foucault, Michel. *The History of Sexuality.* Vintage, New York 1978
Frieze, Irene *et al. Women and Sex Roles.* Norton, New York 1978
Freud, Sigmund. *Inhibitions, Symptoms and Anxiety.* Norton, New York 1959
Goldberg, B. Z. *The Sacred Fire.* Citadel, Secaucus, NJ 1958 (History of sex and religion)
Goldberg, Herb. *The New Male.* Signet, New York 1979
Hite, Shere. *The Hite Report.* Macmillan, New York 1976 (Survey of female sexual attitudes)
Laurence, Theodor. *Satan, Sorcery and Sex.* Parker, West Nyack, New York 1974 (History of sex, religion and superstition)

Marcuse, Herbert. *Eros and Civilization.* Vintage, New York 1955

Rueger, Russ. "Dodging Double Standards Snags," *Gallery,* February 1982

Rueger, Russ. "The Joy of Anomie," *Human Behavior,* April 1973

Rueger, Russ. "Obscenity: The Case for Free Speech," in *Obscenity: Censorship or Free Choice?* Greenleaf, San Diego 1971

Rueger, Russ. "Seeking Freedom from the Male Myth," *Human Behavior,* April 1973

Rueger, Russ. "Sexual Touch," in *The Joy of Touch,* Simon & Schuster, New York 1981

Williams, Juanita, ed. *Psychology of Women.* Norton, New York 1979

Sexual Pleasure

Altman, Carole. "The G-spot Updated," *Gallery's Guide to Great Loving,* Gallery Press, New York 1983

Braun, Saul. *Catalog of Sexual Consciousness.* Grove, New York 1975

Brecher, Ruth and Edward, eds. *An Analysis of Human Sexual Response.* Signet, New York 1966

Caprio, Frank. *How to Solve Your Sex Problems with Self-Hypnosis.* Wilshire, Hollywood, CA 1966

Comfort, Alex. *The Joy of Sex.* Simon & Schuster, New York 1972

Denning, Melita and Osborne Phillips. *The Magick of Sex.* Llewellyn, St. Paul, MN 1982 (Roles, ritual, role-playing, spirituality)

Douglas, Nik and Penny Slinger. *Sexual Secrets.* Destiny, New York 1979 (Excellent compendium of oriental sex techniques)

Garrison, Omar. *Tantra: The Yoga of Sex.* Julian, New York 1983

Greene, Gerald and Caroline. *S-M The Last Taboo: A Study of Sado-Masochism.* Ballantine, New York 1974 (Myth-breaking study of subject; illustrates roles, rituals, creative aggression, dominance/submission)

McCorkle, Locke. *How to Make Love.* Grove, New York 1970 (Oriental, spiritual approach)

Masters, William and Virginia Johnson. *The Pleasure Bond.* Bantam, New York 1976

Mookerjee, Ajit and Madhu Khanna. *The Tantric Way.* New York Graphic Society, Boston 1977

Morin, Jack. *Anal Pleasure and Health.* Down There Press, Burlingame, CA 1981

Rama-Andre. *Sexual Yoga.* Quantum Associates, New York 1974

Rueger, Russ. "America's Newest Pleasure Craze: Adult Video," in *The Pleasure Book.* Gallery Press, New York 1983

Rueger, Russ. "Obscenity: the Case for Free Speech," in *Obscenity: Censorship or Free Choice?* Greenleaf, San Diego 1971

Rueger, Russ. "Substitutes for Normal Sex," *Gallery,* February 1983 (Prostitutes, gadgets, surrogates, mail order, etc.)

Rueger, Russ. "One Week to Perfect Seduction," *Gallery,* June 1983

Watts, Alan. *Nature, Man and Woman.* Vintage, New York 1970

Wilson, Robert. *Sex and Drugs.* Playboy Books, Chicago 1973

Pleasure Products

Butwin, David. "Getting Into Hot Water," *Signature,* November 1983 (Hot tubs, Jacuzzis, mineral springs, etc.)

Douglas, Nik and Penny Slinger. *The Pillow Book.* Destiny, New York 1981

Edmund Scientific Catalog, Barrington, NJ (High-tech to the limits: holograms, psychedelic light shows, biofeedback, etc.)

Fantel, Hans. "Magical Musical Machines," *Gallery,* March 1983

Fantel, Hans. "VCRs: Making Your Own Prime Time," *Gallery,* May 1983

Frazier, Gregory and Beverly. *The Bath Book.* Troubador Press, San Francisco 1973

BIBLIOGRAPHY

"The Great Playboy Sex-Aids Road Test," *Playboy,* March 1978

French, Kimberly. "Body Aids for Massage & Well-Being. Tools that Soothe," *Whole Life Times,* November 1982

Gabree, John. "Entertainment 1983—and Beyond," *Gallery,* March 1983 (High-tech home entertainment and beyond)

Johnson, Tom and Tim Miller. *The Sauna Book.* Harper, New York 1977

Lilly, John. *Deep Self.* Simon & Schuster, New York 1977 (Tranquility tanks)

Maclay, K. T. *Total Beauty Catalog.* Coward, New York 1978

Personal Computing and similar magazines keep you informed on the latest in computer developments

Rueger, Russ. "America's Newest Pleasure Craze: Adult Video," in *The Pleasure Book.* Gallery Press, New York 1973

Rueger, Russ. "Substitutes for Normal Sex," *Gallery,* February 1983 (Gadgets, mail order, masturbation aids, etc.)

Rueger, Russ. "Touch Enhancers," in *The Joy of Touch.* Simon & Schuster, New York 1981

Sharper Image Catalog San Francisco; *Hammacher Schlemmer* Catalog New York. (These and similar catalogs keep you informed about the latest pleasure products)

Signature Magazine (Diner's Club Card publication. This and similar magazines feature stories on the newest pleasure fads and products.)

Swartz, Mimi. "For the Woman Who Has Everything," *Esquire,* July 1980

Takiff, Jonathan. "Ultimate in Home Entertainment," *New York Daily News,* November 17, 1983 (Lead article in section featuring info on robots, laser disks, video games, computers, etc.)

Other Pleasure Pursuits

(see prior section for additional information)

DeBold, Richard and Russel Leaf, eds. *LSD, Man & Society.* Wesleyan University Press, Middletown, CT 1967

Grinspoon, Lester and James Bakalar. *Cocaine, a Drug and Its Social Evolution.* Basic, New York 1976

Horman, Richard and Allan Fox. *Drug Awareness.* Avon, New York 1970

Leary, Tim. *The Politics of Ecstasy.* Paladin, London 1970

Metzner, Ralph, ed. *The Ecstatic Adventure.* Macmillan, New York 1970

Morin, Jack. "Drugs and Anal Eroticism," in *Anal Pleasure and Health.* Down There Press, Burlingame, CA 1981

National Institute of Mental Health. "Students and Drug Abuse," *Today's Education,* March 1969

Psychedelic Review, Vol. 1, No. 2, Fall 1963

Psychedelic Review, No. 6, 1965

Psychedelic Review, No. 10, 1969

Rueger, Russ. "Drugs," in *The Joy of Touch.* Simon & Schuster, New York 1981

Rueger, Russ. "Tripping the Heavy Fantastic," *Human Behavior,* March 1973 (Other-worldly experiences with mystic Carlos Castaneda)

Rueger, Russ. "Postscript to a Bum Trip," *Human Behavior,* November 1973

Shulgin, Alexander. "Profiles of Psychedelic Drugs: 10. DOB," *Journal of Psychactive Drugs* Vol. 13(1) Jan.–Mar. 1981

Watts, Alan. *The Joyous Cosmology.* Vintage, New York 1962

Wilson, Robert. *Sex & Drugs.* Playboy Press, Chicago, 1973

The Politics of Pleasure

The references to this last chapter are intimately connected to everything else in this book. In many respects, they form the foundation of it, the underlying rationale for a pleasure philosophy. Therefore, almost all the other references are relevant to this section. To avoid needless repetition, however, the most relevant other sections are Peak Experiences and Self-Actualization, Pleasure Prohibitions, Work, Friendship and Sexual Attitudes.

Andrews, Lewis and Marvin Karlins. *Requiem for Democracy?* Holt, New York 1971

Baltzell, E. Digby. *The Protestant Establishment: Aristocracy & Caste in America.* Vintage, New York 1964

Berger, Peter and Richard Neuhaus. *Movement and Revolution.* Anchor, New York 1970 (On American radicalism)

Brown, Robert. *The Electronic Invasion.* Rider, New York 1967 (Bugging and debugging technology)

Browne, Harry. *How I Found Freedom in An Unfree World.* Avon, New York 1974 (One man's struggle to achieve an independent life)

Cirino, Robert. *Don't Blame the People: How the News Media Use Bias, Distortion and Censorship to Manipulate Public Opinion.* Vintage, New York 1971

Chomsky, Noam. *American Power and the New Mandarins.* Vintage, New York 1969 (The managerial elite and their influence)

Cooper, David, ed. *To Free A Generation.* Collier, New York 1969 (The prospects of liberation from repression)

Coser, Lewis. *Greedy Institutions.* Free Press, New York 1974 (How organizations stifle employees' private lives)

de Tocqueville, Alexis. *Democracy in America.* Washington Square, New York 1964 ("The tyranny of the majority")

Dexter, Lewis and David Manning, eds. *People, Society and Mass Communications.* Free Press, New York 1964

Domhoff, G. William. *Who Rules America?* Prentice-Hall, Englewood Cliffs, NJ 1967

Douglas, Jack, ed. *Deviance and Respectability.* Basic, New York 1970 (The power to label and pigeonhole people)

Douglas, Jack. *Freedom and Tyranny.* Knopf, New York 1970

Douglas, Mary. *Purity and Danger: An Analysis of Concepts of Pollution and Taboo.* Penguin, Baltimore 1970

Ennis, Bruce. *Prisoners of Psychiatry.* Avon, New York 1972 (How mental health laws can stifle freedom and individuality)

Engels, Frederick. *The Origin of the Family, Private Property and the State.* International Publishers, New York 1970

Ferguson, Marilyn. *The Aquarian Conspiracy.* Tarcher, Los Angeles, 1980 (Futuristic look at possibility for social transformation)

Forer, Lois. *Death of the Law.* McKay, New York 1975 (Judge shows uselessness of law to help social problems)

Fromm, Erich. *Escape From Freedom.* Avon, New York 1969 (The temptations of totalitarianism)

Galbraith, John. *The New Industrial State.* Signet, New York 1967 (Technocracy and freedom)

Glass, John and John Staude. *Humanistic Society.* Goodyear, Pacific Palisades, CA 1972 (The ideal state we need to create)

Harris, Richard. *Freedom Spent: Tales of Tyranny in America.* Little, Brown, Boston 1976 (Personal struggles for rights and justice)

United States Senate. *Hearings before the Select Committee to Study Governmental Operations with Respect to Intelligence Activities.* (Multivolume set documenting abuses of IRS, CIA, FBI, etc.)

Heinlein, Robert. *Stranger in a Strange Land.* Avon, New York 1961 (Fictional account of killing of an alien who came to Earth to spread message of love and pleasure)

Henry, Jules. *Culture Against Man.* Vintage, New York 1963

Hirsch, Sherry *et al. Madness Network News Reader.* Glide, San Francisco 1974 (Ex-mental patients tell of abuse of system)

Hitler, Adolf. *Mein Kampf.* Houghton Mifflin, Boston 1943

Hoffman, Paul. *Lions in the Street.* Saturday Review Press, New York 1973 (Power of big law firms and their Fortune 500 clients)

Kahn, Si. *How People Get Power: Organizing Oppressed Communities for Action.* McGraw-Hill, New York 1970

Key, Wilson. *Subliminal Seduction.* Signet, New York 1973 (How hidden symbols in ads manipulate people)

Keyes, Ken. *The Hundredth Monkey,* Vision Books, Coos Bay, OR 1981 (Prospects for a nuclear holocaust and what you can do to prevent it)

Kittrie, Nicholas. *The Right to Be Different: Deviance and Enforced Therapy.* Johns Hopkins University Press, Baltimore 1971 (How the psychiatric and other power elites stifle individualism and free thinking)

Kuhn, Thomas. *The Structure of Scientific Revolutions.* University of Chicago Press, Chicago 1970 (How scientific elites prevent new theories from gaining acceptance or recognition)

Lasch, Christopher. *The Culture of Narcissism.* Norton, New York 1978 (The selfish, destructive, "Me Generation" philosophy dissected)

Lawrence, D. H. *Sex, Literature and Censorship.* Viking, New York 1959

Lefcourt, Robert, ed. *Law Against the People.* Vintage, New York 1971 (Demystification of the courts as arenas for justice)

Leonard, George. *Education and Ecstasy.* Dell, New York 1968 (How education *could* be under an enlightened philosophy)

Leonard, George. *The Transformation.* Dell, New York 1972 (Futuristic view of human transformation)

Lundberg, Ferdinand. *The Rich and the Super-Rich.* Bantam, New York 1968 (The ultimate power of big bucks)

Marcuse, Herbert. *An Essay on Liberation.* Beacon, Boston 1969

Marcuse, Herbert. *Eros and Civilization.* Vintage, New York 1955 (How culture represses our natural instincts and pleasure drives)

Marcuse, Herbert. *One-Dimensional Man.* Beacon, Boston 1966 (The narrow niche that industrialism forces most of us into)

McCormick, John and Mairi MacInnes, eds. *Versions of Censorship.* Anchor, New York 1962 (Views of some of the world's great thinkers)

Miller, Perry, ed. *The American Puritans.* Anchor, New York 1956

Mills, C. Wright. *Power, Politics and People.* Oxford, New York 1967

Mische, Gerald and Patricia. *Toward a New World Order.* Paulist Press, New York 1977 (Optimistic visions of the dawn of a New Age)

Ney, Richard. *The Wall Street Gang.* Praeger, New York 1974 (Power of the financial monarchs)

Official Report of the National Commission on the Causes and Prevention of Violence. *Rights in Conflict.* NAL, New York 1968 (The Chicago police riot during the Democratic Convention demonstrations in 1968. An example of what happens when the power structure feels threatened)

Packard, Vance. *The Hidden Persuaders.* Pocket, New York 1966 (How the admen trick you into buying their wares)

Penal Code of the State of New York. Looseleaf Law Pubs., New York 1976 (Typical of the laws of the fifty states regarding repressive sexual, mental health, drug, etc., statutes. Most rarely used but they're always there if needed)

Powers, Ron. *The News-Casters: News Business as Show Business.* St. Martin's Press, New York 1977 (More media manipulation)

Reich, Wilhelm. *The Mass Psychology of Fascism.* Farrar, New York 1970

Report of the Commission on Obscenity and Pornography. Bantam, New York 1970 (Legalization recommendations soundly rejected by repressive establishment)

Robbins, Rossell. *Encyclopedia of Witchcraft and Demonology.* Crown, New York 1959 (Shows the absurdity to which the power elite will go to repress perceived threats: burnings, torture, racks, etc.)

Roszack, Theodore. *The Making of a Counter Culture.* Anchor, NY 1969

Rueger, Russ *et al. Book of the Strange.* Signet, New York 1977

Rueger, Russ. "The Graduate Student As Nigger," *New University,* October 15, 1974 (The games and conformity of graduate education)

Rueger, Russ. "The Ghetto," *Third World,* Spring 1971 (Minority oppression)

Rueger, Russ. "Libertarianism: the Alternative Revolution," *New University,* November 25, 1970

Rueger, Russ. "The Men's Movement," *Sherwood Forest,* May/June 1974

Rueger, Russ. "The Men's Movement 1974," *WIN,* April 1974

Rueger, Russ. "The Need for Men's Liberation," *Sherwood Forest* November 1971

Rueger, Russ. "A New Freedom," *Richmond Times,* December 18, 1969

Rueger, Russ. "Obscenity: The Case for Free Speech," in *Obscenity: Censorship or Free Choice?* Greenleaf, San Diego 1971

Rueger, Russ. "Out of Work Islander Fights the System," *Staten Island Register,* November 20, 1975

Rueger, Russ. "Phenomenological Sociology: Issues and Applications," *Phenomenological Sociology,* August 1974 (Academic freedom)

Rueger, Russ. "Plight of the Unemployed Ph.D.," *Seed,* February 1976

Rueger, Russ. "Postscript to a Bum Trip," *Human Behavior,* November 1973

Rueger, Russ. "Psychological Freedom," *New University,* April 9, 1971

Rueger, Russ. "Premonitions of a Police State," *Dolphin,* January 3, 1968

Rueger, Russ. "Repression East and West," *New University,* October 7, 1970

Rueger, Russ. "Scholarly Thoughts," *Student Lawyer,* February 1981 (Exposé of the repressive law school education and the tyrannical legal job market)

Rueger, Russ. "Seeking Freedom From the Male Myth," *Human Behavior,* April 1973

Rueger, Russ. "Solzhenitsn: Of the People," *New University,* May 28, 1971

Rueger, Russ. "The Taft Street Story," *Staten Island Register,* August 17, 1972 (Minority oppression through poor housing)

Rueger, Russ. "Three Faces of Being: Toward an Existential Psychology," *Phenomenological Sociology,* November 1973

Rueger, Russ. "Tyranny and Technology," *New University* October 25, 1974

Rueger, Russ. "The Unmaking of a Dissident," *Madness Network News,* Spring 1978 (Blatant psychiatric abuse to stifle a dissident's writing)

Rueger, Russ. "The Way of Alan Watts," *New University,* May 21, 1971

Rueger, Russ. "Wake Up and Live," *Dolphin,* December 6, 1967

Ryan, William. *Blaming the Victim.* Vintage, New York 1971 (How the powerful castes blame and shame the poor and powerless)

Santa Clara Lawyer: Symposium. Mental Illness, The Law and Civil Liberties. Spring 1973 (Experts examine blatant psychiatric abuses)

Skinner, B. F. *Beyond Freedom & Dignity.* Bantam, New York 1971 (Leading behaviorist exposes plan to control human actions and volition)

Sonenblick, Jerry. *The Legality of Love.* Jove, New York 1981

Szasz, Thomas. *The Manufacture of Madness: A Comparative Study of the Inquisition and the Mental Health Movement.* Harper, New York 1970

Toffler, Alvin. *The Third Wave.* Morrow, New York 1980 (Futurist look at available human alternatives)

Trotsky, Leon. *Literature and Revolution.* University of Michigan, Ann Arbor 1971

Veblen, Thorstein. *The Theory of the Leisure Class.* Mentor, New York 1953

Weber, Max. *The Protestant Ethic and the Spirit of Capitalism.* Scribners, New York 1958

Wheeler, Stanton. *On Record: Files and Dossiers in American Life.* Russell Sage, New York 1969 (Privacy? Read this classic)

Whyte, William. *The Organization Man.* Anchor, New York 1956 (Classic study of corporate conformism)

Wolff, Robert *et al. A Critique of Pure Tolerance.* Beacon, Boston, 1969 (The establishment allows a certain amount of criticism until it feels threatened, then the iron fist comes out of the velvet glove.)

TAPES, RECORDS AND OTHER RELATED MATERIALS
1. Instructional, Inspirational, Educational Tapes and Other Aids

Association for Research & Enlightenment, Sixty-Seventh Street and Atlantic Avenue, P.O. Box 595, Virginia Beach, VA 23451 (800-368-2727) (Metaphysical books and tapes, especially Edgar Cayce materials)

Automated Learning, 1275 Bloomfield Avenue, Fairfield, NJ 07006 (Hypnotism, metaphysical, relaxation, educational, success)

Eric Butterworth Cassette Tapes, Unity Center, 143 West Fifty-First Street, New York, NY 10019 (Inspirational, success, prosperity from mystical Christian view)

Coleman Publishing, 99 Milbur Boulevard, Farmingdale, NY 11735 (Metaphysical books on tape, including *Course in Miracles*)

Co-Creative Productions, 2512 San Pablo Avenue, Berkeley, CA 94702 (Interviews with spiritual leaders)

Discovering Success, 163 West Twenty-Third Street, New York, NY 10011 (Success, motivation)

Edmund Scientific Catalog, 101 East Gloucester Pike, Barrington, NJ 08007 (Besides high-tech pleasure products, includes astronomy tapes and audio-visual cassettes)

Esalen Tapes, Big Sur Recordings, P.O. Box 91, Big Sur, CA 93920 (Human potential, psychedelic, psychosis, spiritual, psychology)

Golden Keys Success Seminars, P.O. Box 9358, Salt Lake City, Utah 84109 (Success, prosperity, abundance)

Good Vibes, P.O. Box 32413, Fridley, MN 55432 (Success tapes, but they also carry crystals, pyramids and other magical aids)

Himalayan Institute, RD-1, Box 88-A, Honesdale, PA 18431 (Large selection of metaphysical and spiritual books and cassettes)

Holistic Health Resource Catalog, P.O. Box 20037, Seattle, WA 98102 (New Age music and relaxation tapes, plus health books and products)

Vernon Howard, New Life, Box 684, Boulder City, NV 89005 (Inspirational, spiritual tapes and books)

Impossible Possibilities, 238 West Street, Annapolis, MD 21403 (Trance teachings on spiritual subjects from ancient China)

Institute of Human Development, P.O. Box 41165, Cincinnati, OH 45241 (Spiritual teachings from Jonathan Parker; New Age music)

ISHK Book Service, P.O. Box 176, Los Altos, CA 94022 (Psychology, spirituality from leading thinkers like Idries Shah, Robert Ornstein)

Ken Keyes Center, 790 Commercial Avenue, Coos Bay, OR 97420 (Tapes and books on Universal Love, spirituality and enlightenment)

Kripalu Center, Box 106H, Summit Station, PA 17979 (Yoga, meditation, massage tables, spiritual books)

Life Unlimited, 8125 Sunset, Suite 204, Fair Oaks, CA 95628 (New Age books and tapes; success, prosperity, rebirthing, Rev. Ike tapes)

Lindisfarne Press, R.D. #2, West Stockbridge, MA 01266 (Books and tapes on New Age, esoteric, occult)

Llewellyn Pubs., P.O. Box 43383-834, St. Paul, MN 55164 (Astrology, magic, occult, herbology books and tapes)

Lorian Press, P.O. Box 147, Middleton, WI 53562 (New Age music, esoteric, futuristic, spiritual tapes and books)

Love Tapes, Effective Learning Systems, 6950 France Avenue South, Suite 14, Edina, MN 55435 (Hypnosis, music, New Age books, vitamins)

Mystical Rose: New Age Tools & Toys, Box 38, Malibu, CA 90265 (Bold attempt to bring together many of the other programs and products listed here. Tapes, books, products, music, etc.)

Metavisions, 2067 Broadway, Suite 27, New York, NY 10023 (Tapes on healing, vision improvement by Martin Brofman)

Nightingale-Conant Corp., 3730 West Devon Avenue, Chicago, IL 60659 (800-323-5552) (Tape programs on management, success, prosperity, winning)

Jeffrey Norton Publishers, Suite 78N On-The-Green, Guilford, CT 06437 (Tapes by seminal thinkers like Castaneda, Skinner, Watts, Freud, Frost)

Pathmark Tapes, P.O. Box 7251, Grand Rapids, MI 49510 (Occult, mystic, meditation, prayer, numerology, spiritual)

Planet Tapes, Box 9128, Morristown, NJ 07960 (Leading thinkers like Capra, Pearce, Szasz, Grof, Lilly, Ram Dass, Ferguson, Laing)

Potentials Unlimited, 4808-H Broadmoor, Grand Rapids, MI 49508 (While focus still basically on self-improvement by hypnosis, now includes books on tape, music, video programs, language tapes, books)

Psychology Today Cassettes, Dept. A0833, P.O. Box 278, Pratt Station, Brooklyn, NY 11205 (Stress, worry, communication, therapy, depression, pain)

Publishers Central Bureau, Dept. 225, One Champion Way, Avenel, NJ 07001 (Besides one of the largest selections of discounted books, music and instruction tapes; video films)

Rainbow's End, 8130 Big Bend Boulevard, Webster Groves, MO 63119 (New Age tapes and music, books, products, vitamins, exercisers, pyramids)

Reb Dovid Din Tapes, Alvin Feinstein, 661 Morton Avenue, Franklin Square, NY 11010 (Kabbalah, Jewish mysticism, biblical study)

Rev. Ike Tapes, G.P.O. Box 50, New York, NY 10116 (Prosperity, success)

Self-Centered Tapes, 876B Highway 35, Middletown, NJ 07748 (Love, relaxation, hypnosis fear, stress, creativity)

Seth Corporation, P.O. Box 934, Van Nuys, CA 91408 (Endless loop tapes for visualization, affirmations, music, breathing, learning)

Success Motivation Institute, 5000 Lakewood Drive, Waco, TX 76710 (Management, success, prosperity, psychology, books on tape, power)

Soundworks, 1912 North Lincoln Street, Arlington, VA 22207 (800-422-0111) (Seminal thinkers like Ferguson, LeBoyer, Fuller, Erhard)

Summit Lighthouse, Box A, Malibu, CA 90265 (Esoteric, mystical, religious books and tapes; New Age music)

Taylor-Made Pubs., Dept. 62-OM, 1441-A Walnut Street, Berkeley CA 94709 (Immortality, healing, prosperity, inspiration tapes and books)

Tans-Com, P.O. Box 8097, Waco, TX 76714 (800-433-3314) (Personal improvement, success, sales, management, inspiration tapes and books)

Uniquity, 215 Fourth Street, P.O. Box 6, Galt, CA 95632 (Growth products, exercisers, games, books and tapes on psychology, education, recreation)

Unity Cassettes, Unity Village, MO 64065 (Religion, inspiration, prosperity, meditation, books and tapes)

University of the Trees Press, P.O. Box 66, Boulder Creek, CA 95006 (Spirituality, nutrition, meditation, healing, books and tapes.

Alan Watts Institute, P.O. Box 361, Mill Valley, CA 94942 (Tapes, books by noted spiritual teacher)

2. Music

While many of the above also included music, the following specialize in New Age, healing, meditation and nature sound tapes.

GRD Recordings, P.O. Box 13054, Phoenix, AZ 85002

East-West Books, 78 Fifth Avenue, New York, NY 10011 "Music for the New Age" Catalog

The New Age Music Catalog, Vital Body Marketing, P.O. Box 703, Fresh Meadows, NY 11365 (800-221-0200)

Soundings of the Planet, P.O. Box 43512, Tucson, AZ 85733

3. Miscellaneous

Expando-Vision, Stimutech, P.O. Box 2575, Dept. 301 F. E. Lansing, MI 48823 (Self-improvement through videocassette tapes. Please note that some of the other listings above also offer videotape programs. This is an area bound to explode soon.)

Planetary Citizens, 777 United Nations Plaza, New York, NY 10017 (Books, posters, community organizations, guides, tapes, audio-visual aides, with the themes of futurism, nuclear disarmament, peace, world unity)

Smile Herb Shop's Gifts and Treasures, 4908 Berwyn Road, College Park, MD 20740 (Mail order for herbs, teas, soaps, mugs, books, etc.)

Deva, Box W83, Burkittsville, MD 21718 (Makers of all-natural-fiber clothing like drawstring pants, shorts, etc. Excellent for yoga or exercise, comfortable, nonbinding, good for circulation)

Hot Tub catalog, California Cooperage, P.O. Box E, San Luis Obispo, CA 93406

Massage/bodywork tables, Oakworks, 21300 Heathcote Road, Freeland, MD 21053 (Catalog available)

(Also see listings above and under "pleasure products" in other section of bibliography)

No inference is intended that this reference list is in any way complete. There are plenty of equally good products, books and tapes made by other manufacturers that have not come to my attention. Admittedly, the weakest listing is for music, because the bulk of my file was taken by a student. But most of the information on the nonbook references came from space ads or classified ads in publications like *New Age, Whole Life Times, East-West Journal* and the like. Any pleasure philosopher would find it well worth his time to visit a local metaphysical bookstore and become familiar with publications like these. The old order was puritanical, while the freethinkers constituting the New Age movement are definitely propleasure.

Both the panties and bras are in pink,
and they're cut so's to make o man think!
(If you give him a chance
Both the bra and the pants
will come off just as quick as a wink!)